12 Sermons
on the
Lord's Supper

Charles H. Spurgeon

BAKER

Reprinted 1994 by Baker Book House Company

Published by Baker Books
a division of Baker Book House Company
P.O. Box 6287, Grand Rapids, MI 49516-6287

Printed in the United States of America

ISBN 0-8010-8393-1

Sermons were selected from *"Till He Come" :*
Communion Meditations and Addresses by C. H. Spurgeon,
 published by Marshall, Morgan & Scott, Ltd.

Contents

"The cup of blessing which we bless, is it not the communion of the blood of Christ? The bread which we break, is it not the communion of the body of Christ? For we being many are one bread, and one body : for we are all partakers of that one bread."—1 *Cor.* x. 16, 17.

1

Communion with Christ and His People

I WILL read you the text as it is given in the Revised Version: "The cup of blessing which we bless, is it not a communion of the blood of Christ?" That is to say,—Is it not one form of expressing the communion of the blood of Christ? "The bread," or as it is in the margin, "the loaf which we break, is it not a communion of the body of Christ? seeing that we, who are many, are one loaf, one body: for we all partake of the one loaf." The word "loaf" helps to bring out more clearly the idea of unity intended to be set forth by the apostle.

It is a lamentable fact that some have fancied that this simple ordinance of the Lord's supper has a certain magical, or at least physical power about it, so that, by the mere act of eating and drinking this bread and wine, men can be made partakers of the body and blood of Christ. It is marvellous that so plain a symbol should have been so complicated by genuflexions, adornments, and technical phrases. Can anyone see the slightest resemblance between the Master's sitting down with the twelve, and the mass of the Roman community? The original rite is lost in the super-imposed ritual. Superstition has produced a sacrament where Jesus intended a fellowship. Too many, who would not go the length of Rome, yet speak of this simple feast as if it were a mystery dark and obscure. They employ all manner of hard words to turn the children's bread into a stone. It is not the Lord's supper, but the Eucharist; we see before us no plate, but a "paten"; the cup is a "chalice", and the table is an "altar." These are incrustations of superstition, whereby 'the blessed ordinance of Christ is likely to be again overgrown and perverted.

What does this supper mean? It means communion: *communion with Christ, and communion with one another.*

What is communion? The word breaks up easily into union, and its prefix *com*, which means *with*, union with. We must, therefore, first enjoy union with Christ, and with His Church, or else we cannot enjoy communion. Union lies at the basis of communion. We must be one with Christ in heart, and soul, and life; baptized into His death; quickened by His life, and so brought to be members of His body, one with the whole Church of which He is the Head. We cannot have communion with Christ till we are in union with *Him;* and we cannot have communion with the Church till we are in vital union with *it.*

I. The teaching of the Lord's supper is just this —that while we have many ways of COMMUNION WITH CHRIST, yet the receiving of Christ into our souls as our Saviour is the best way of communion with Him.

I said, dear friends, that we have many ways of communion with Christ; let me show you that it is so.

Communion is ours *by personal intercourse* with the

Lord Jesus. We speak with Him in prayer, and He speaks with us through the Word. Some of us speak oftener with Christ than we do with wife or child, and our communion with Jesus is deeper and more thorough than our fellowship with our nearest friend. In meditation and its attendant thanksgiving we speak with our risen Lord, and by His Holy Spirit He answers us by creating fresh thought and emotion in our minds. I like sometimes in prayer, when I do not feel that I can say anything, just to sit still, and look up; then faith spiritually descries the Well-beloved, and hears His voice in the solemn silence of the mind. Thus we have intercourse with Jesus of a closer sort than any words could possibly express. Our soul melts beneath the warmth of Jesus' love, and darts upward her own love in return. Think not that I am dreaming, or am carried off by the memory of some unusual rhapsody : no, I assert that the devout soul can converse with the Lord Jesus all the day, and can have as true fellowship with Him as if He still dwelt bodily among men. This thing comes to me, not by the hearing of the ear, but by my own personal experience : I know of a surety that Jesus manifests Himself unto His people as He doth not unto the world.

Ah, what sweet communion often exists between the saint and the Well-beloved, when there is no bread and wine upon the table, for the Spirit Himself draws the heart of the renewed one, and it runs after Jesus, while the Lord Himself appears unto the longing spirit! Truly our fellowship is with the Father, and with His Son Jesus Christ. Do *you* enjoy this charming converse?

Next, we have communion with Christ *in His thoughts, views, and purposes ;* for His thoughts are our thoughts according to our capacity and sanctity. Believers take the same view of matters as Jesus does ; that which pleases Him pleases them, and that which grieves Him grieves them also. Consider, for instance, the greatest theme of our thought, and see whether our thoughts are not like those of Christ. He delights in the Father, He loves to glorify the Father : do not we ? Is not the Father the centre of our soul's delight ? Do we not rejoice at the very sound of His name ? Does not our spirit cry, " Abba, Father " ? Thus it is clear we feel as Jesus feels towards the Father, and so we have the truest communion with Him. This is but one instance ; your contemplations will bring before you a wide variety of topics wherein we think with Jesus. Now, identity of judgment, opinion, and purpose forms the highway of communion ; yea, it is communion.

We have also communion with Christ *in our emotions.* Have you never felt a holy horror when you have heard a word of blasphemy in the street ? Thus Jesus felt when He saw sin, and bore it in His own person : only He felt it infinitely more than you do. Have you never felt as you looked upon sinners that you must weep over them ? Those are holy tears, and contain the same ingredients as those which Jesus shed when He lamented over Jerusalem. Yes, in our zeal for God, our hatred of sin, our detestation of falsehood, our pity for men, we have true communion with Jesus.

Further, we have had fellowship with Christ *in many of our actions.* Have you ever tried to teach the

8

ignorant? This Jesus did. Have you found it difficult? So Jesus found it. Have you striven to reclaim the backslider? Then you were in communion with the Good Shepherd who hastens into the wilderness to find the one lost sheep, finds it, lays it upon His shoulders, and brings it home rejoicing. Have you ever watched over a soul night and day with tears? Then you have had communion with Him who has borne all our names upon His broken heart, and carries the memorial of them upon His pierced hands. Yes, in acts of self-denial, liberality, benevolence, and piety, we enter into communion with Him who went about doing good. Whenever we try to disentangle the snarls of strife, and to make peace between men who are at enmity, then are we doing what the great Peace-maker did, and we have communion with the Lord and Giver of peace. Whereever, indeed, we co-operate with the Lord Jesus in His designs of love to men, we are in true and active communion with Him.

So it is *with our sorrows*. Certain of us have had large fellowship with the Lord Jesus in affliction. "Jesus wept": He lost a friend, and so have we. Jesus grieved over the hardness of men's hearts: we know that grief. Jesus was exceedingly sorry that the hopeful young man turned away, and went back to the world: we know that sorrow. Those who have sympathetic hearts, and live for others, readily enter into the experience of "the Man of sorrows." The wounds of calumny, the reproaches of the proud, the venom of the bigoted, the treachery of the false, and the weakness of the true, we have known in our measure; and therein have had communion with our Lord Jesus.

Nor this alone : we have been with our Divine Master *in His joys.* I suppose there never lived a happier man than the Lord Jesus. He was rightly called " the Man of sorrows " ; but He might, with un-impeachable truth, have been called, " the Man of joys." He must have rejoiced as He called His disciples, and they came unto Him ; as He bestowed healing and relief ; as He gave pardon to penitents, and breathed peace on believers. His was the joy of finding the sheep, and taking the piece of money out of the dust. His work was His joy : such joy that, for its sake, He endured the cross, despising the shame. The exercise of benevolence is joy to loving hearts : the more pain it costs, the more joy it is. Kind actions make us happy, and in such joy we find communion with the great heart of Jesus.

Thus have I given you a list of windows of agate and gates of carbuncle through which you may come at the Lord ; but the ordinance of the Lord's supper sets forth a way which surpasses them all. It is the most accessible and the most effectual method of fellowship. Here it is that we have fellowship with the Lord Jesus by receiving Him as our Saviour. We, being guilty, accept of His atonement as our sacrificial cleansing, and in token thereof we eat this bread and drink this cup. " Oh ! " says one, " I do not feel that I can get near to Christ. He is so high and holy, and I am only a poor sinner." Just so. For that very reason you can have fellowship with Christ in that which lies nearest to His heart : He is a Saviour, and to be a Saviour there must be a sinner to be saved. Be you that one, and Christ and you shall at once be in union and communion : He shall save, and you shall be saved ; He shall sanctify, and you shall be sanctified ; and twain shall thus be one. This table sets before you His great sacrifice. Jesus has offered it ; will you accept it? He does not ask you to bring anything,—no drop of blood, no pang of flesh ; all is here, and your part is to come and partake of it, even as of old the offerer partook of the peace-offering which he had brought, and so feasted with God and with the priest. If you work for Christ, that will certainly be some kind of fellowship with Him ; but I tell you that the communion of receiving him into your inmost soul is the nearest and closest fellowship possible to mortal man. The fellowship of service is exceedingly honourable, when we and Christ work together for the same objects ; the fellowship of suffering is exceedingly instructive, when our heart has graven upon it the same characters as were graven upon the heart of Christ : but the fellowship of the soul which receives Christ, and is received by Christ, is closer, more vital, more essential than any other.

Such fellowship is eternal. No power upon earth can henceforth take from me the piece of bread which I have just now eaten, it has gone where it will be made up into blood, and nerve, and muscle, and bone. It is within me, and of me. That drop of wine has coursed through my veins, and is part and parcel of my being. So he that takes Jesus by faith to be his Saviour has chosen the good part which shall not be taken away from him. He has received the Christ into his inward parts, and all the men on earth, and all the devils in hell, cannot extract Christ from him. Jesus saith, " He that eateth Me, even he shall live by

Me." By our sincere reception of Jesus into our hearts, an indissoluble union is established between us and the Lord, and this manifests itself in mutual communion. To as many as received Him, to them has He given this communion, even to them that believe on His name.

II. I have now to look at another side of communion,—namely, the FELLOWSHIP OF TRUE BELIEVERS WITH EACH OTHER. We have many ways of communing the one with the other, but there is no way of mutual communing like the common reception of the same Christ in the same way. I have said that there are many ways in which Christians commune with one another, and these doors of fellowship I would mention at some length.

Let me go over much the same ground as before. We commune by *holy converse*. I wish we had more of this. Time was when they that feared the Lord spake often one to another ; I am afraid that now they more often speak one against another. It is a grievous thing that full often love lies bleeding by a brother's hand. Where we are not quite so bad as that, yet we are often backward and silent, and so miss profitable converse. Our insular reserve has often made one Christian sit by another in utter isolation, when each would have been charmed with the other's company. Children of one family need not wait to be introduced to each other : having eaten of this one bread, we have given and received the token of brotherhood ; let us therefore act consistently with our relationship, and fall into holy conversation next time we meet. I am afraid that Christian brotherhood in many cases begins and ends inside the place of worship. Let it not be so among us. Let it be our delight to find our society in the circle of which Jesus is the centre, and let us make those our friends who are the friends of Jesus. By frequent united prayer and praise, and by ministering the one to the other the things which we have learned by the Spirit, we shall have fellowship with each other in our Lord Jesus Christ.

I am sure that all Christians have fellowship together in their *thoughts.* In the essentials of the gospel we think alike : in our thoughts of God, of Christ, of sin, of holiness, we keep step ; in our intense desire to promote the kingdom of our Lord, we are as one. All spiritual life is one. The thoughts raised by the Spirit of God in the souls of men are never contrary to each other. I say not that the thoughts of all professors agree, but I do assert that the minds of the truly regenerate in all sects, and in all ages, are in harmony with each other,—a harmony which often excites delighted surprise in those who perceive it. The marks that divide one set of nominal Christians from another set are very deep and wide to those who have nothing of religion but the name ; yet living believers scarcely notice them. Boundaries which separate the cattle of the field are no division to the birds of the air. Our minds, thoughts, desires, and hopes are one in Christ Jesus, and herein we have communion.

Beloved friends, our *emotions* are another royal road of fellowship. You sit down and tell your experience, and I smile to think that you are telling mine. Sometimes a young believer enlarges upon the sad story of his trials and temptations, imagining that nobody ever had to endure so great a fight, when all the while he is only describing the common adventures of those who go on pilgrimage, and we are all communing with him. When we talk together about our Lord, are we not agreed? When we speak of our Father, and all His dealings with us, are we not one? And when we weep, and when we sigh, and when we sing, and when we rejoice, are we not all akin? Heavenly fingers touching like strings within our hearts bring forth the self-same notes, for we are the products of the same Maker, and tuned to the same praise. Real harmony exists among all the true people of God : Christians are one in Christ.

We have communion with one another, too, in our *actions.* We unite in trying to save men : I hope we do. We join in instructing, warning, inviting, and persuading sinners to come to Jesus. Our life-ministry is the same : we are workers together with God. We live out the one desire,—"Thy kingdom come. Thy will be done in earth, as it is in heaven."

Certainly we have much communion one with the other in our *sufferings.* There is not a poor sick or despondent saint upon the earth with whom we do not sympathize at this moment, for we are fellow-members, and partakers of the sufferings of Christ. I hope we can say,—

> " Is there a lamb in all Thy flock,
>   I would disdain to feed?
> Is there a foe, before whose face,
>   I fear Thy cause to plead? "

No, we suffer with each other, and bear each other's burden, and so fulfil the law of Christ. If we do not, we have reason for questioning our own

14

faith; but if we do so, we have communion with each other.

I hope we have fellowship in our *joys*. Is one happy? We would not envy him, but rejoice with him. Perhaps this is not so universal as it should be among professors. Are we at once glad because another prospers? If another star outshines ours, do we delight in its radiance? When we meet a brother with ten talents, do we congratulate ourselves on having such a man given to help us, or do we depreciate him as much as we can? Such is the depravity of our nature, that we do not readily rejoice in the progress of others if they leave us behind; but we must school ourselves to this. A man will speedily sit down and sympathize with a friend's griefs; but if he sees him honoured and esteemed, he is apt to regard him as a rival, and does not so readily rejoice with him. This ought not to be; without effort we ought to be happy in our brother's happiness. If we are ill, be this our comfort, that many are in robust health; if we are faint, let us be glad that others are strong in the Lord. Thus shall we enjoy a happy fellowship like that of the perfected above.

When I have put all these modes of Christian communion together, no one of them is so sure, so strong, so deep, as communion in receiving the same Christ as our Saviour, and trusting in the same blood for cleansing unto eternal life. Here on the table you have the tokens of the broadest and fullest communion. This is a kind of communion which you and I cannot choose or reject: if we are in Christ, it is and must be ours. Certain brethren restrict their communion in

the outward ordinance, and they think they have good
reasons for doing so ; but I am unable to see the force
of their reasoning, because I joyfully observe that
these brethren commune with other believers in
prayer, and praise, and hearing of the Word, and other
ways : the fact being that the matter of real communion is very largely beyond human control, and is
to the spiritual body what the circulation of the blood
is to the natural body, a necessary process not
dependent upon volition. In perusing a deeply
spiritual book of devotion, you have been charmed
and benefited, and yet upon looking at the title-page
it may be you have found that the author belonged
to the Church of Rome. What then ? Why, then it
has happened that the inner life has broken all
barriers, and your spirits have communed. For my
own part, in reading certain precious works, I have
loathed their Romanism, and yet I have had close
fellowship with their writers in weeping over sin, in
adoring at the foot of the cross, and in rejoicing in
the glorious enthronement of our Lord. Blood is
thicker than water, and no fellowship is more inevitable
and sincere than fellowship in the precious blood, and
in the risen life of our Lord Jesus Christ. Here, in the
common reception of the one loaf, we bear witness
that we are one ; and in the actual participation of all
the chosen in the one redemption, that unity is in very
deed displayed and matured in the most substantial
manner. Washed in the one blood, fed on the same
loaf, cheered by the same cup, all differences pass
away, and " we, being many, are one body in Christ,
and every one members one of another."

Now, then, dear friends, if this kind of fellowship be

the best, LET US TAKE CARE TO ENJOY IT. Let us at this hour avail ourselves of it.

Let us take care to *see Christ* in the mirror of this ordinance. Have any of you eaten the bread, and yet have you not seen Christ? Then you have gained no benefit. Have you drunk the wine, but have you not remembered the Lord? Alas! I fear you have eaten and drunk condemnation to yourselves, not discerning the Lord's body. But if you did see through the emblems, as aged persons see through their spectacles, then you have been thankful for such aids to vision. But what is the use of glasses if there is nothing to look at? and what is the use of the communion if Christ be not in our thoughts and hearts?

If you did discern the Lord, then be sure, again, to *accept Him.* Say to yourself, " All that Christ is to any, He shall be to me. Does He save sinners? He shall save me. Does He change men's hearts? He shall change mine. Is He all in all to those that trust Him? He shall be all in all to me." I have heard persons say that they do not know how to take Christ. What says the apostle? " The Word is nigh thee, even in thy mouth, and in thy heart." If you have something in your mouth that you desire to eat, what is the best thing to do? Will you not swallow it? That is exactly what faith does. Christ's word of grace is very near you, it is on your tongue; let it go down into your inmost soul. Say to your Saviour, " I know I am not fit to receive Thee, O Jesus, but since Thou dost graciously come to me as bread comes to the hungry, I thankfully receive Thee, rejoicing to feed upon Thee! Since Thou dost come to me as the fruit of the vine to a thirsty man, Lord, I take Thee, willingly, and I thank Thee that this reception is all that Thou dost require of me. Has not Thy Spirit so put it—' As many as received Him, to them gave He power to become the sons of God, even to them that believe on His name'?"

Beloved friends, when you have thus received Jesus, fail not to *rejoice in Him* as having received Him. How many there are who have received Christ, who talk and act as if they never had received Him! It is a poor dinner of which a man says, after he has eaten it, that he feels as if he had not dined ; and it is a poor Christ of whom anyone can say, " I have received Him, but I am none the happier, none the more at peace." If you have received Jesus into your heart, you *are* saved, you *are* justified. Do you whisper, "I hope so"? Is that all? Do you not know? The hopings and hoppings of so many are a poor way of going ; put both feet down, and say, " I know whom I have believed, and am persuaded that He is able to keep that which I have committed unto Him against that day." You are either saved or lost ; there is no state between the two. You are either pardoned or condemned ; and you have good reason for the highest happiness, or else you have grave causes for the direst anxiety. If you have received the atonement, be as glad as you can be ; and if you are still an unbeliever, rest not till Christ is yours.

Oh, the joy of continually entering into fellowship with Christ, in such a way that you never lose His company! Be this yours, beloved, every day, and all the day! May His shadow fall upon you as you rest in the sun, or stray in the gardens! May His voice cheer you as you lie down upon the sea-shore, and listen to the murmuring of the waves; may His presence glorify the mountain solitude as you climb the hills! May Jesus be to you an all-surrounding presence, lighting up the night, perfuming the day, gladdening all places, and sanctifying all pursuits! Our Beloved is not a Friend for Lord's-days only, but for week-days, too; He is the inseparable Companion of His loving disciples. Those who have had fellowship with His body and His blood at this table may have the Lord as an habitual Guest at their own tables; those who have met their Master in this upper room may expect Him to make their own chamber bright with His royal presence. Let fellowship with Jesus and with the elect brotherhood be henceforth the atmosphere of our life, the joy of our existence. This will give us a heaven below, and prepare us for a heaven above.

"And when they had sung an hymn, they went out into the mount of Olives."—*Matthew* xxvi. 30.

2

The Memorable Hymn

THE occasion on which these words were spoken
was the last meal of which Jesus partook in
company with His disciples before He went from them
to His shameful trial and His ignominious death. It
was His farewell supper before a bitter parting, and
yet they needs must sing. He was on the brink of
that great depth of misery into which He was about
to plunge, and yet He would have them sing "an
hymn." It is wonderful that HE sang, and in a
second degree it is remarkable that THEY sang. We
will consider both singular facts.

I. Let us dwell a while on THE FACT THAT JESUS
SANG AT SUCH A TIME AS THIS. What does He
teach us by it? Does He not say to each of us, His
followers, "*My religion is one of happiness and joy;
I, your Master, by My example would instruct you
to sing even when the last solemn hour is come, and
all the glooms of death are gathering around you?*
Here, at the table, I am your Singing-master, and set
you lessons in music, in which My dying voice shall
lead you: notwithstanding all the griefs which over-
whelm My heart, I will be to you the Chief Musician,
and the Sweet Singer of Israel"? If ever there was
a time when it would have been natural and consistent
with the solemnities of the occasion for the Saviour to
have bowed His head upon the table, bursting into a

flood of tears ; or, if ever there was a season when He might have fittingly retired from all company, and have bewailed His coming conflict in sighs and groans, it was just then. But no ; that brave heart will sing "an hymn." Our glorious Jesus plays the man beyond all other men. Boldest of the sons of men, He quails not in the hour of battle, but tunes His voice to loftiest psalmody. The genius of that Christianity of which Jesus is the Head and Founder, its object, spirit, and design, are happiness and joy, and they who receive it are able to sing in the very jaws of death.

This remark, however, is quite a secondary one to the next : *our Lord's complete fulfilment of the law is even more worthy of our attention.* It was customary, when the Passover was held, to sing, and this is the main reason why the Saviour did so. During the Passover, it was usual to sing the hundred and thirteenth, and five following Psalms, which were called the "*Hallel.*" The first commences, you will observe, in our version, with "Praise ye the Lord !" or, "Hallelujah !" The hundred and fifteenth, and the three following, were usually sung as the closing song of the Passover. Now, our Saviour would not diminish the splendour of the great Jewish rite, although it was the last time that He would celebrate it. No ; there shall be the holy beauty and delight of psalmody ; none of it shall be stinted ; the "Hallel" shall be full and complete. We may safely believe that the Saviour sang through, or probably chanted, the whole of these six Psalms; and my heart tells me that there was no one at the table who sang more devoutly or more cheerfully than did our blessed Lord. There are some parts of the hundred and eighteenth Psalm, especially, which strike us as having sounded singularly grand, as they flowed from His blessed lips. Note verses 22, 23, 24. Particularly observe those words, near the end of the Psalm, and think you hear the Lord Himself singing them, "God is the Lord, which hath shewed us light: bind the sacrifice with cords, even unto the horns of the altar. Thou art my God, and I will praise Thee: Thou art my God, I will exalt Thee. O give thanks unto the Lord; for He is good: for His mercy endureth for ever."

Because, then, it was the settled custom of Israel to recite or sing these Psalms, our Lord Jesus Christ did the same; for He would leave nothing unfinished. Just as, when He went down into the waters of baptism, He said, "Thus it becometh us to fulfil all righteousness," so He seemed to say, when sitting at the table, "Thus it becometh us to fulfil all righteousness; therefore let us sing unto the Lord, as God's people in past ages have done." Beloved, let us view with holy wonder the strictness of the Saviour's obedience to His Father's will, and let us endeavour to follow, in His steps, in all things, seeking to be obedient to the Lord's Word in the little matters as well as in the great ones.

May we not venture to suggest another and deeper reason? Did not the singing of "an hymn" at the supper show *the holy absorption of the Saviour's soul in His Father's will?* If, beloved, you knew that at —say ten o'clock to-night—you would be led away to be mocked, and despised, and scourged, and that to-morrow's sun would see you falsely accused, hanging, a convicted criminal, to die upon a cross, do you think that you could sing to-night, after your last meal? I am sure you could not, unless with more than earth-born courage and resignation your soul could say, "Bind the sacrifice with cords, even unto the horns of the altar." You would sing if your spirit were like the Saviour's spirit; if, like Him, you could exclaim, "Not as I will, but as Thou wilt;" but if there should remain in you any selfishness, any desire to be spared the bitterness of death, you would not be able to chant the "Hallel" with the Master. Blessed Jesus, how wholly wert Thou given up! how perfectly consecrated! so that, whereas other men sing when they are march-ing to their joys, Thou didst sing on the way to death; whereas other men lift up their cheerful voices when honour awaits them, Thou hadst a brave and holy sonnet on Thy lips when shame, and spitting, and death were to be Thy portion.

This singing of the Saviour also teaches us *the whole-heartedness of the Master in the work which He was about to do.* The patriot-warrior sings as he hastens to battle; to the strains of martial music he advances to meet the foeman; and even thus the heart of our all-glorious Champion supplies Him with song even in the dreadful hour of His solitary agony. He views the battle, but He dreads it not; though in the contest His soul will be "exceeding sorrowful even unto death," yet before it, He is like Job's war-horse, "he saith among the trumpets, Ha, ha; and he smelleth the battle afar off." He has a baptism to be baptized with, and He is straitened until it be accomplished. The Master does not go forth to the agony in the garden with a cowed and trembling spirit, all bowed and crushed in the dust, but He

advances to the conflict like a man who has his full
strength about him —taken out to be a victim (if I
may use such a figure), not as a worn-out ox that has
long borne the yoke, but as the firstling of the bullock,
in the fulness of His strength. He goes forth to the
slaughter, with His glorious undaunted spirit fast and
firm within Him, glad to suffer for His people's sake.
and for His Father's glory.

> " For as at first Thine all-pervading look
>   Saw from Thy Father's bosom to th' abyss,
>   Measuring in calm presage
>   The infinite descent ;
>   So to the end, though now of mortal pangs
>   Made heir, and emptied of Thy glory a while,
>   With unaverted eye
>   Thou meetest all the storm."

Let us, O fellow-heirs of salvation, learn to sing when
our suffering time comes, when our season for stern
labour approaches ; ay, let us pour forth a canticle of
deep, mysterious, melody of bliss, when our dying hour
is near at hand ! Courage, brother ! The waters are
chilly ; but fear will not by any means diminish the
terrors of the river. Courage, brother ! Death is
solemn work ; but playing the coward will not make
it less so. Bring out the silver trumpet ; let thy lips
remember the long-loved music, and let the notes be
clear and shrill as thou dippest thy feet in the Jordan :
" Yea, though I walk through the valley of the shadow
of death, I will fear no evil: for Thou art with me ;
Thy rod and Thy staff they comfort me." Dear friends,
let the remembrance of the melodies of that upper
room go with you to-morrow into business ; and if
you expect a great trial, and are afraid you will not

be able to sing after it, then sing before it comes. Get your holy praise-work done before affliction mars the tune. Fill the air with music while you can. While yet there is bread upon the table, sing, though famine may threaten ; while yet the child runs laughing about the house, while yet the flush of health is in your own cheek, while yet your goods are spared, while yet your heart is whole and sound, lift up your song of praise to the Most High God ; and let your Master, the singing Saviour, be in this your goodly and comfortable example.

There is much more that might be said concerning our Lord's sweet swan-song, but there is no need to crowd one thought out with another ; your leisure will be well spent in meditation upon so fruitful a theme.

II. We will now consider THE SINGING OF THE DISCIPLES. *They* united in the " Hallel "—like true Jews, they joined in the national song. Israel had good cause to sing at the Passover, for God had wrought for His people what He had done for no other nation on the face of the earth. Every Hebrew must have felt his soul elevated and rejoiced on the Paschal night. He was " a citizen of no mean city ", and the pedigree which he could look back upon was one, compared with which kings and princes were but of yesterday.

Remembering the fact commemorated by the Paschal supper, Israel might well rejoice. They sang of their nation in bondage, trodden beneath the tyrannical foot of Pharaoh ; they began the Psalm right sorrowfully, as they thought of the bricks made without straw, and of the iron furnace ; but the strain soon mounted from the deep bass, and began to climb the scale, as they sang of Moses the servant of God, and of the Lord appearing to him in the burning bush. They remembered the mystic rod, which became a serpent, and which swallowed up the rods of the magicians; their music told of the plagues and wonders which God had wrought upon Zoan; and of that dread night when the first-born of Egypt fell before the avenging sword of the angel of death, while they themselves, feeding on the lamb which had been slain for them, and whose blood was sprinkled upon the lintel and upon the side-posts of the door, had been graciously preserved. Then the song went up concerning the hour in which all Egypt was humbled at the feet of Jehovah, whilst as for His people, He led them forth like sheep, by the hand of Moses and Aaron, and they went by the way of the sea, even of the Red Sea. The strain rose higher still as they tuned the song of Moses, the servant of God, and of the Lamb. Jubilantly they sang of the Red Sea, and of the chariots of Pharaoh which went down into the midst thereof, and the depths covered them till there was not one of them left. It was a glorious chant indeed when they sang of Rahab cut in pieces, and of the dragon wounded at the sea, by the right hand of the Most High, for the deliverance of the chosen people.

But, beloved, if I have said that Israel could so properly sing, *what shall I say of those of us who are the Lord's spiritually redeemed?* We have been emancipated from a slavery worse than that of Egypt: "with a high hand and with an outstretched arm," hath God delivered us. The blood of Jesus Christ, the Lamb of God's Passover, has been sprinkled on

our hearts and consciences. By faith we keep the
Passover, for we have been spared ; we have been
brought out of Egypt ; and though our sins did once
oppose us, they have all been drowned in the Red Sea
of the atoning blood of Jesus: "the depths have
covered them, there is not one of them left." If the
Jew could sing a "great Hallel", our "Hallel" ought
to be more glowing still ; and if every house in
"Judæa's happy land" was full of music when the
people ate the Paschal feast, much more reason have
we for filling every heart with sacred harmony to-
night, while we feast upon Jesus Christ, who was
slain, and has redeemed us to God by His blood.

III. The time has now come for me to say HOW
EARNESTLY I DESIRE YOU TO "SING AN HYMN."

I do not mean to ask you to use your voices,
but let your hearts be brimming with the essence of
praise. Whenever we repair to the Lord's table, which
represents to us the Passover, we ought not to come
to it as to a funeral. Let us select solemn hymns, but
not dirges. Let us sing softly, but none the less joyfully. These are no burial feasts ; those are not
funeral cakes which lie upon this table, and yonder
fair white linen cloth is no winding-sheet. "This is
My body," said Jesus, but the body so represented
was no corpse , we feed upon a living Christ. The
blood set forth by yonder wine is the fresh life-blood
of our immortal King. We view not our Lord's body
as clay-cold flesh, pierced with wounds, but as glorified
at the right hand of the Father. We hold a happy
festival when we break bread on the first day of the
week. We come not hither trembling like bondsmen,
cringing on our knees as wretched serfs condemned to

eat on their knees; we approach as freemen to our Lord's banquet, like His apostles, to recline at length or sit at ease; not merely to eat bread which may belong to the most sorrowful, but to drink wine which belongs to men whose souls are glad. Let us recognize the rightness, yea, the duty of cheerfulness at this commemorative supper; and, therefore, let us "sing an hymn."

Being satisfied on this point, perhaps you ask, "*What hymn shall we sing?*" Many sorts of hymns were sung in the olden time: look down the list, and you will scarcely find one which may not suit us now.

One of the earliest of earthly songs was *the war-song*. They sang of old a song to the conqueror, when he returned from the battle. "Saul has slain his thousands, and David his ten thousands." Women took their timbrels, and rejoiced in the dance when the hero returned from the war. Even thus of old did the people of God extol Him for His mighty acts, singing aloud with the high-sounding cymbals: "Sing unto the Lord, for He hath triumphed gloriously . . . The Lord is a man of war: the Lord is His name." My brethren, let us lift up a war-song to-night! Why not? "Who is this that cometh from Edom, with dyed garments from Bozrah? this that is glorious in His apparel, travelling in the greatness of His strength? I that speak in righteousness, mighty to save." Come, let us praise our Emmanuel, as we see the head of our foe in His right hand; as we behold Him leading captivity captive, ascending up on high, with trumpets' joyful sound, let us chant the pæan; let us shout the war-song, "*Io Triumphe!*" Behold, He comes, all glorious from the war: as we gather at this

festive table, which reminds us both of His conflict
and of His victory, let us salute Him with a psalm of
gladsome triumph, which shall be but the prelude of
the song we expect to sing when we get up—

<blockquote>"Where all the singers meet."</blockquote>

Another early form of song was *the pastoral*. When
the shepherds sat down amongst the sheep, they tuned
their pipes, and warbled forth soft and sweet airs in
harmony with rustic quietude. All around was calm
and still; the sun was brightly shining, and the birds
were making melody among the leafy branches.
Shall I seem fanciful if I say, let us unite in a pastoral
to-night? Sitting round the table, why should we
not sing, "The Lord is my Shepherd; I shall not
want. He maketh me to lie down in green pastures:
He leadeth me beside the still waters"? If there be
a place beneath the stars where one might feel
perfectly at rest and ease, surely it is at the table of
the Lord. Here, then, let us sing to our great
Shepherd a pastoral of delight. Let the bleating of
sheep be in our ears as we remember the Good
Shepherd who laid down His life for His flock.

You need not to be reminded that the ancients
were very fond of *festive songs*. When they assembled
at their great festivals, led by their chosen minstrels,
they sang right joyously, with boisterous mirth. Let
those who will speak to the praise of wine, my soul
shall extol the precious blood of Jesus; let who will
laud corn and oil, the rich produce of the harvest, my
heart shall sing of the Bread which came down from
heaven, whereof, if a man eateth, he shall never hunger.
Speak ye of royal banquets, and minstrelsy fit for a

monarch's ear? Ours is a nobler festival, and our song is sweeter far. Here is room at this table to-night for all earth's poesy and music, for the place deserves songs more lustrous with delight, more sparkling with gems of holy mirth, than any of which the ancients could conceive.

> " Now for a tune of lofty praise
> To great Jehovah's equal Son !
> Awake, my voice, in heavenly lays
> Tell the loud wonders He hath done ! "

The *love-song* we must not forget, for that is peculiarly the song of this evening. " Now will I sing unto my Well-beloved a song." His love to us is an immortal theme ; and as our love, fanned by the breath of heaven, bursts into a vehement flame, we may sing, yea, and we will sing among the lilies, a song of loves.

In the Old Testament, we find many Psalms called by the title, " *A Song of Degrees*." This " Song of Degrees " is supposed by some to have been sung as the people ascended the temple steps, or made pilgrimages to the holy place. The strain often changes, sometimes it is dolorous, and anon it is gladsome ; at one season, the notes are long drawn out and heavy, at another, they are cheerful and jubilant. We will sing a " Song of Degrees " to-night. We will mourn that we pierced the Lord, and we will rejoice in pardon bought with blood. Our strain must vary as we talk of sin, feeling its bitterness, and lamenting it, and then of pardon, rejoicing in its glorious fulness.

David wrote a considerable number of Psalms which he entitled, " *Maschil*," which may be called in English, "instructive Psalms." Where, beloved, can we find richer instruction than at the table of our Lord? He who understands the mystery of incarnation and of substitution, is a master in Scriptural theology. There is more teaching in the Saviour's body and in the Saviour's blood than in all the world besides. O ye who wish to learn the way to comfort, and how to tread the royal road to heavenly wisdom, come ye to the cross, and see the Saviour suffer, and pour out His heart's blood for human sin!

Some of David's Psalms are called, "*Michtam*". which means "golden Psalm." Surely we must sing one of these. Our psalms must be golden when we sing of the Head of the Church, who is as much fine gold. More precious than silver or gold is the inestimable price which He has paid for our ransom. Yes, ye sons of harmony, bring your most melodious anthems here, and let your Saviour have your golden psalms!

Certain Psalms in the Old Testament are entitled, "*Upon Shoshannim*," that is, "Upon the lilies." O ye virgin souls, whose hearts have been washed in blood, and have been made white and pure, bring forth your instruments of song :—

> " Hither, then, your music bring,
> Strike aloud each cheerful string! "

Let your hearts, when they are in their best state, when they are purest, and most cleansed from earthly dross, give to Jesus their glory and their excellence.

Then there are other Psalms which are dedicated "*To the sons of Korah.*" If the guess be right, the reason why we get the title, "To the sons of Korah "

32

—" a song of loves"—must be this : that when Korah,
Dathan, and Abiram were swallowed up, the sons of
Dathan and Abiram were swallowed up, too ; but the
sons of Korah perished not. Why they were not
destroyed, we cannot tell. Perhaps it was that
sovereign grace spared those whom justice might have
doomed ; and " the sons of Korah " were ever after
made the sweet singers of the sanctuary ; and whenever there was a special " song of loves", it was always
dedicated to them. Ah! we will have one of those
songs of love to-night, around the table, for we, too, are
saved by distinguishing grace. We will sing of the
heavenly Lover, and the many waters which could not
quench His love.

> " Love, so vast that nought can bound ;
> Love, too deep for thought to sound
> Love, which made the Lord of all
> Drink the wormwood and the gall.
>
> " Love, which led Him to the cross,
> Bearing there unutter'd loss ;
> Love, which brought Him to the gloom
> Of the cold and darksome tomb.
>
> " Love, which made Him hence arise
> Far above the starry skies,
> There with tender, loving care,
> All His people's griefs to share.
>
> " Love, which will not let Him rest
> Till His chosen all are blest ;
> Till they all for whom He died
> Live rejoicing by His side."

We have not half exhausted the list, but it is clear
that, sitting at the Lord's table, we shall have no lack
of suitable psalmody. Perhaps no one hymn will quite

meet the sentiments of all ; and while we would not write a hymn for you, we would pray the Holy Spirit to write now the spirit of praise upon your hearts, that, sitting here, you may " after supper " sing "an hymn."

IV. For one or two minutes let us ask,—" WHAT SHALL THE TUNE BE?" It must be a strange one, for if we are to sing "an hymn" to-night, around the table, the tune must have all the parts of music. Yonder believer is heavy of heart through manifold sorrows, bereavements, and watchings by the sick. He loves his Lord, and would fain praise Him, but his soul refuses to use her wings. Brother, we will have a tune in which you can join, and you shall lead the bass. You shall sing of your fellowship with your Beloved in His sufferings ; how He, too, lost a friend ; how He spent whole nights in sleeplessness ; how His soul was exceeding sorrowful. But the tune must not be all bass, or it would not suit some of us to-night, for we can reach the highest note. We have seen the Lord, and our spirit has rejoiced in God our Saviour. We want to lift the chorus high ; yea, there are some true hearts here who are at times so full of joy that they will want special music written for them. " Whether in the body, I cannot tell ; or whether out of the body, I cannot tell:" said Paul, and so have said others since, when Christ has been with them. Ah ! then they have been obliged to mount to the highest notes, to the very loftiest range of song.

Remember, beloved, that the same Saviour who will accept the joyful shoutings of the strong, will also receive the plaintive notes of the weak and weeping. You little ones, you babes in grace, may cry,

"Hosanna," and the King will not silence you; and you strong men, with all your power of faith, may shout, "Hallelujah!" and your notes shall be accepted, too.

Come, then, let us have a tune in which we can all unite; but ah! we cannot make one which will suit the dead—the dead, I mean, "in trespasses and sins"—and there are some such here. Oh, may God open their mouths, and unloose their tongues; but as for those of us who are alive unto God, let us, as we come to the table, all contribute our own share of the music, and so make up a song of blended harmony, with many parts, one great united song of praise to Jesus our Lord!

We should not choose a tune for the communion table which is not very *soft*. These are no boisterous themes with which we have to deal when we tarry here. A bleeding Saviour, robed in a vesture dyed with blood—this is a theme which you must treat with loving gentleness, for everything that is coarse is out of place. While the tune is soft, it must also be *sweet*. Silence, ye doubts; be dumb, ye fears; be hushed, ye cares! Why come ye here? My music must be sweet and soft when I sing of Him. But oh! it must also be *strong*; there must be a full swell in my praise. Draw out the stops, and let the organ swell the diapason! In fulness let its roll of thundering harmony go up to heaven; let every note be sounded at its loudest. "Praise ye Him upon the cymbals, upon the high-sounding cymbals; upon the harp with a solemn sound." Soft, sweet, and strong, let the music be.

Alas! you complain that your soul is out of tune. Then ask the Master to tune the heart-strings. Those "Selahs" which we find so often in the Psalms, are supposed by many scholars to mean, " Put the harp-strings in tune : " truly we require many " Selahs ", for our hearts are constantly unstrung. Oh, that to-night the Master would enable each one of us to offer that tuneful prayer which we so often sing,—

> " Teach me some melodious sonnet,
>   Sung by flaming tongues above :
>   Praise the mount—oh, fix me on it,
>   Mount of God's unchanging love ! "

V. We close by enquiring,—WHO SHALL SING THIS HYMN ?

Sitting around the Father's board, we will raise a joyful song, but who shall do it ? " I will," saith one ; " and we will," say others. What is the reason why so many are willing to join ? The reason is to be found in the verse we were singing just now,—

> " When He's the subject of the song,
>   Who can refuse to sing ? "

What ! a Christian silent when others are praising his Master ? No ; he must join in the song. Satan tries to make God's people dumb, but he cannot, for the Lord has not a tongue-tied child in all His family. They can all speak, and they can all cry, even if they cannot all sing, and *I* think there are times when they can all sing ; yea, they must, for you know the promise, " Then shall the tongue of the dumb sing." Surely, when Jesus leads the tune, if there should be any silent ones in the Lord's family, they must begin to praise the name of the Lord. After Giant Despair's head had been cut off, Christiana and Mr. Greatheart, and all the rest of them, brought out the best of their provisions, and made a feast, and Mr. Bunyan says that, after they had feasted, they danced. In the dance there was one remarkable dancer, namely, Mr. Ready-to-Halt. Now, Mr. Ready-to-Halt usually went upon crutches, but for once he laid them aside. "And," says Bunyan, "I warrant you he footed it well!" This is quaintly showing us that, sometimes, the very sorrowful ones, the Ready-to-Halts, when they see Giant Despair's head cut off, when they see death, hell, and sin led in triumphant captivity at the wheels of Christ's victorious chariot, feel that even *they* must for once indulge in a song of gladness. So, when I put the question to-night, "Who will sing?" I trust that Ready-to-Halt will promise, "I will."

You have not much comfort at home, perhaps; by very hard work you earn that little. Sunday is to you a day of true rest, for you are worked very cruelly all the week. Those cheeks of yours, poor girl, are getting very pale, and who knows but what Hood's pathetic lines may be true of you?—

> "Stitch, stitch, stitch,
>   In poverty, hunger, and dirt,
>   Sewing at once, with a double thread,
>   A shroud as well as a shirt."

But, my sister, you may surely rejoice to-night in spite of all this. There may be little on earth, but there is much in heaven. There may be but small comfort for you here apart from Christ; but oh! when, by faith, you mount into His glory, your soul is glad. You shall be as rich as the richest to-night if the Holy Spirit shall but bring you to the table, and enable you to feed upon your Lord and Master. Perhaps you have come here to-night when you ought not to have done so. The physician would have told you to keep to your bed, but you persisted in coming up to the house where the Lord has so often met with you. I trust that we shall hear your voice in the song. There appear to have been in David's day many things to silence the praise of God, but David was one who would sing. I like that expression of his, where the devil seems to come up, and put his hand on his mouth, and say, "Be quiet." "No," says David, "I will sing." Again the devil tries to quiet him, but David is not to be silenced, for three times he puts it, "I will sing, yea, I will sing praises unto the Lord." May the Lord make you resolve this night that you will praise the Lord Jesus with all your heart!

Alas! there are many of you here to-night whom I could not invite to this feast of song, and who could not truly come if you were invited. Your sins are not forgiven; your souls are not saved; you have not trusted Christ; you are still in nature's darkness, still in the gall of bitterness, and in the bonds of iniquity. Must it always be so? Will you destroy yourselves? Have you made a league with death, and a covenant with hell? Mercy lingers! Longsuffering continues! Jesus waits! Remember that He hung upon the cross for sinners such as you are, and that if you believe in Him now, you shall be saved. One act of faith, and all the sin you have committed is blotted out. A single glance of faith's eye to the wounds of the Messiah, and your load of iniquity is rolled into the depths of the sea, and you are forgiven in a moment!

"Oh!" says one, "would God I could believe!" Poor soul may God help thee to believe now! God took upon Himself our flesh; Christ was born among

men, and suffered on account of human guilt, being
made to suffer " the Just for the unjust, that He might
bring us to God." Christ was punished in the room,
place, and stead of every man and woman who will
believe on Him. If you believe on Him, He was
punished for you ; and you will never be punished.
Your debts are paid, your sins are forgiven. God
cannot punish you, for He has punished Christ instead
of you, and He will never punish twice for one offence.
To believe is to trust. If you will now trust your soul
entirely with Him, you are saved, for He loved you,
and gave Himself for you. When you know this, and
feel it to be true, then come to the Lord's table,
and join with us, when, AFTER SUPPER WE SING OUR
HYMN,—

> "' It is finished !'—Oh, what pleasure
>   Do these charming words afford !
> Heavenly blessings without measure
>   Flow to us from Christ the Lord :
>   ' It is finished ! '
>   Saints, the dying words record.
>
> "Tune your harps anew, ye seraphs,
>   Join to sing the pleasing theme ;
> All on earth, and all in heaven,
>   Join to praise Immanuel's name '
>   Hallelujah !
>   Glory to the bleeding Lamb ' '

" And He was in the hinder part of the ship, asleep on a pillow: **and** they awake Him, and say unto Him, Master, carest Thou not that **we** perish? And He arose, and rebuked the wind, and said unto the **sea,** Peace, be still. And the wind ceased, and there was a great calm."— *Mark* iv. 38, 39.

3

Jesus Asleep on a Pillow

OUR Lord took His disciples with Him into the ship to teach them a practical lesson. It is one thing to talk to people about our oneness with them, and about how they should exercise faith in time of danger, and about their real safety in apparent peril; but it is another, and a far better thing, to go into the ship with them, to let them feel all the terror of the storm, and then to arise, and rebuke the wind, and say unto the sea, "Peace, be still." Our Lord gave His disciples a kind of Kindergarten lesson, an acted sermon, in which the truth was set forth visibly before them. Such teaching produced a wonderful effect upon their lives. May we also be instructed by it!

In our text there are two great calms; the first is, *the calm in the Saviour's heart*, and the second is, *the calm which He created* with a word upon the storm-tossed sea.

1. WITHIN THE LORD THERE WAS A GREAT CALM, and that is why there was soon a great calm around Him; for what is in God comes out of God. Since there was a calm in Christ for Himself, there was afterwards a calm outside for others. What a wonderful inner calm it was! "He was in the hinder part of the ship, asleep on a pillow."

He had *perfect confidence in God* that all was well. The waves might roar, the winds might rage, but He was not at all disquieted by their fury. He knew that the waters were in the hollow of His Father's hand, and that every wind was but the breath of His Father's mouth; and so He was not troubled; nay, He had not even a careful thought, He was as much at ease as on a sunny day. His mind and heart were free from every kind of care, for amid the gathering tempest He deliberately laid Himself down, and slept like a weary child. He went to the hinder part of the ship, most out of the dash of the spray; He took a pillow, and put it under His head, and with fixed intent disposed Himself to slumber. It was His own act and deed to go to sleep in the storm; He had nothing for which to keep awake, so pure and perfect was His confidence in the great Father. What an example this is to us! We have not half the confidence in God that we ought to have, not even the best of us. The Lord deserves our unbounded belief, our unquestioning confidence, our undisturbed reliance. Oh, that we rendered it to Him as the Saviour did!

There was also mixed with His faith in the Father *a sweet confidence in His own Sonship.* He did not doubt that He was the Son of the Highest. I may not question God's power to deliver, but I may sometimes question my right to expect deliverance; and if so, my comfort vanishes. Our Lord had no doubts of this kind. He had long before heard that word, " This is My beloved Son, in whom I am well pleased ; " He had so lived and walked with God that the witness within Him was continuous, so He had no question about the Father's love to Him as His own Son. " Rocked in the cradle of the deep," His Father keeping watch over Him,—what could a child do better than go to sleep in such a happy position? And so He does. You and I, too, want a fuller assurance of our sonship if we would have greater peace with God. The devil knows that, and therefore he will come to us with his insinuating suggestion, " If thou be the son of God." If we have the Spirit of adoption in us, we shall put the accuser to rout at once, by opposing the Witness within to his question from without. Then shall we be filled with a great calm, because we have confidence in our Father, and assurance of our sonship.

Then *He had a sweet way*—this blessed Lord of ours—*of leaving all with God*. He takes no watch, He makes no fret ; but He goes to sleep. Whatever comes, He has left all in the hands of the great Caretaker ; and what more is needful? If a watchman were set to guard my house, I should be foolish if I also sat up for fear of thieves. Why have a watchman if I cannot trust him to watch? "Cast thy burden upon the Lord ; " but when thou hast done so, leave it with the Lord, and do not try to carry it thyself. That is to make a mock of God, to have the name of God, but not the reality of God. Lay down every care, even as Jesus did when He went calmly to the hinder part of the ship, and quietly took a pillow, and went to sleep.

But I think I hear someone say, " I could do that if mine were solely care about myself." Yes, perhaps you could ; and yet you cannot cast upon God your burden of care about your children. But your Lord trusted the Father with those dear to Him. Do you not think that Christ's disciples were as precious to Him as our children are to us? If that ship had been wrecked, what would have become of Peter? What would have become of "that disciple whom Jesus loved"? Our Lord regarded with intense affection those whom He had chosen and called, and who had been with Him in His temptation, yet He was quite content to leave them all in the care of His Father, and go to sleep.

You answer, "Yes, but there is a still wider circle of people watching to see what will happen to me, and to the cause of Christ with which I am connected. I am obliged to care, whether I will or no." Is your case, then, more trying than your Lord's? Do you forget that "there were also with Him many other little ships"? When the storm was tossing His barque, their little ships were even more in jeopardy; and He cared for them all. He was the Lord High Admiral of the Lake of Gennesaret that night. The other ships were a fleet under His convoy, and His great heart went out to them all. Yet He went to sleep, because He had left in His Father's care even the solicitudes of His charity and sympathy. We, my brethren, who are much weaker than He, shall find strength in doing the same.

Having left everything with His Father, *our Lord did the very wisest thing possible.* He did just what the hour demanded. "Why," say you, " He went to sleep!" That was the best thing Jesus could do; and sometimes it is the best thing we can do. Christ was weary and worn; and when anyone is exhausted, it is his duty to go to sleep if he can. The Saviour must be up again in the morning, preaching and working miracles, and if He does not sleep, He will not be fit for His holy duty; it is incumbent upon

44

Him to keep Himself in trim for His service. Knowing that the time to sleep has come, the Lord sleeps, and does well in sleeping. Often, when we have been fretting and worrying, we should have glorified God far more had we literally gone to sleep. To glorify God by sleep is not so difficult as some might think ; at least, to our Lord it was natural. Here you are worried, sad, wearied ; the doctor prescribes for you ; his medicine does you no good ; but oh ! if you enter into full peace with God, and go to sleep, you will wake up infinitely more refreshed than by any drug. The sleep which the Lord giveth to His beloved is balmy indeed. Seek it as Jesus sought it. Go to bed, brother, and you will better imitate your Lord than by putting yourself into ill humour, and worrying other people.

There is a spiritual sleep in which we ought to imitate Jesus. How often I have worried my poor brain about my great church, until I have come to my senses, and then I have said to myself, " How foolish you are ! Can you not depend upon God ? Is it not far more His cause than yours ? " Then I have taken my load in prayer, and left it with the Lord. I have said, " In God's name, this matter shall never worry me again," and I have left my urgent care with Him, and ended it for ever. I have so deliberately given up many a trying case into the Lord's care that, when any of my friends have said to me, " What about so and so ? " I have simply answered, " I do not know, and I am no longer careful to know. The Lord will interpose in some way or other, but I will trouble no more about it." No mischief has ever come through any matter which I have left in the divine keeping. The staying of my hand has been wisdom. "Stand still, and see the salvation of God," is God's own precept. Here let us follow Jesus. Having a child's confidence in the great Father, He retires to the stern of the ship, selects a pillow, deliberately lies down upon it, and goes to sleep; and though the ship is filling with water, and rolls and pitches, He sleeps on. Nothing can break the peace of His tranquil soul. Every sailor on board reels to and fro, and staggers like a drunken man, and is at his wits' end; but Jesus is neither at his wits' end, nor does He stagger, for He rests in perfect innocence, and undisturbed confidence. His heart is happy in God, and therefore doth He remain in repose. Oh, for grace to copy Him!

II. But here notice, dear friends, THE DIFFERENCE BETWEEN THE MASTER AND HIS DISCIPLES; for while He was in a great calm, they were in a great storm. Here see their failure. They were just as we are, and we are often just as they were.

They gave way to fear. They were sorely afraid that the ship would sink, and that they would all perish. In thus yielding to fear, *they forgot the solid reasons for courage which lay near at hand;* for, in truth, they were safe enough. Christ is on board that vessel, and if the ship goes down, He will sink with them. The heathen mariner took courage during a storm from the fact that Cæsar was on board the ship that was tossed by stormy winds; and should not the disciples feel secure with Jesus on board? Fear not, ye carry Jesus and His cause! Jesus had come to do a work, and His disciples might have known that He could not perish with that work unaccomplished. Could

46

they not trust Him? They had seen Him multiply the loaves and fishes, and cast out devils, and heal all manner of sicknesses; could they not trust Him to still the storm? Unreasonable unbelief! Faith in God is true prudence, but to doubt God is irrational. It is the height of absurdity and folly to question omnipotent love.

And *the disciples were so unwise as to do the Master a very ill turn.* He was sadly weary, and sorely needed sleep; but they hastened to Him, and aroused Him in a somewhat rough and irreverent manner. They were slow to do so, but their fear urged them; and therefore they awoke Him, uttering ungenerous and unloving words : " Master, carest Thou not that we perish?" Shame on the lips that asked so harsh a question! Did they not upon reflection greatly blame themselves? He had given them no cause for such hard speeches; and, moreover, it was unseemly in them to call Him "Master," and then to ask Him, " Carest Thou not that we perish?" Is He to be accused of such hard-heartedness as to let His faithful disciples perish when He has power to deliver them? Alas, we, too, have been guilty of like offences! I think I have known some of Christ's disciples who have appeared to doubt the wisdom or the love of their Lord. They did not quite say that He was mistaken, but they said that He moved in a mysterious way; they did not quite complain that He was unkind to them, but they whispered that they could not reconcile His dealings with His infinite love. Alas, Jesus has endured much from our unbelief! May this picture help us to see our spots, and may the love of our dear Lord remove them !

47

III.   I have spoken to you of the Master's calm and of the disciples' failure; now let us think of THE GREAT CALM WHICH JESUS CREATED. "There was a great calm."

His voice produced it. They say that if oil be poured upon the waters they will become smooth, and I suppose there is *some* truth in the statement; but there is all truth in this, that if God speaks, the storm subsides into a calm, so that the waves of the sea are still. It only needs our Lord Jesus to speak in the heart of any one of us, and immediately the peace of God, which passeth all understanding, will possess us. No matter how drear your despondency, nor how dread your despair, the Lord can at once create a great calm of confidence. What a door of hope this opens to any who are in trouble! If I could speak a poor man rich, and a sick one well, I am sure I would do so at once; but Jesus is infinitely better than I am, and therefore I know that He will speak peace to the tried and troubled heart.

Note, too, that *this calm came at once.* "Jesus arose, and rebuked the wind, and said unto the sea, Peace, be still. And the wind ceased, and there was a great calm." As soon as Jesus spake, all was quiet. I have met with a very large number of persons in trouble of mind, and I have seen a few who have slowly come out into light and liberty; but more frequently deliverance has come suddenly. The iron gate has opened of its own accord, and the prisoner has stepped into immediate freedom. "The snare is broken, and we are escaped." What a joy it is to know that rest is so near even when the tempest rages most furiously!

48

Note, also, that *the Saviour coupled this repose with faith,* for He said to the disciples as soon as the calm came, " Why are ye so fearful? How is it that ye have no faith?" Faith and the calm go together. If thou believest, thou shalt rest; if thou wilt but cast thyself upon thy God, surrendering absolutely to His will, thou shalt have mercy, and joy, and light. Even if we have no faith, the Lord will sometimes give us the blessing that we need, for He delights to do more for us than we have any right to expect of Him; but usually the rule of His kingdom is, " According to your faith be it unto you."

This great calm is very delightful, and concerning this I desire to bear my personal testimony. I speak from my own knowledge when I say that it passeth all understanding. I was sitting, the other night, meditating on God's mercy and love, when suddenly I found in my own heart a most delightful sense of perfect peace. I had come to Beulah-land, where the sun shines without a cloud. " There was a great calm." I felt as mariners might do who have been tossed about in broken water, and all on a sudden, they cannot tell why, the ocean becomes as unruffled as a mirror, and the sea-birds come and sit in happy circles upon the water. I felt perfectly content, yea, undividedly happy. Not a wave of trouble broke upon the shore of my heart, and even far out to sea in the deeps of my being all was still. I knew no ungratified wish, no unsatisfied desire. I could not discover a reason for uneasiness, or a motive for fear. There was nothing approaching to fanaticism in my feelings, nothing even of excitement: my soul was waiting upon God, and delighting herself alone in

Him. Oh, the blessedness of this rest in the Lord! What an Elysium it is! I must be allowed to say a little upon this purple island in the sea of my life: it was none other than a fragment of heaven. We often talk about our great spiritual storms, why should we not speak of our great calms? If ever we get into trouble, what a noise we make of it! Why should we not sing of our deliverances?

Let us survey our mercies. Every sin that we have ever committed is forgiven. "The blood of Jesus Christ, His Son, cleanseth us from all sin." The power of sin within us is broken; it "shall not have dominion over you, for ye are not under the law but under grace." Satan is a vanquished enemy; the world is overcome by our Lord Jesus, and death is abolished by Him. All providence works for our good. Eternity has no threat for us, it bears within its mysteries nothing but immortality and glory. Nothing can harm us. The Lord is our shield, and our exceeding great reward. Wherefore, then, should we fear? The Lord of hosts is with us, the God of Jacob is our refuge. To the believer, peace is no presumption: he is warranted in enjoying "perfect peace"—a quiet which is deep, and founded on truth, which encompasses all things, and is not broken by any of the ten thousand disturbing causes which otherwise might prevent our rest. "Thou wilt keep him in perfect peace whose mind is stayed on Thee; because he trusteth in Thee." Oh, to get into that calm, and remain in it till we come to that world where there is no more sea!

A calm like that which ruled within our Saviour should we be happy enough to attain to it will give us in our measure the power to make outside matters calm. He that hath peace can make peace. We cannot work miracles, and yet the works which Jesus did shall we do also. Sleeping His sleep, we shall awake in His rested energy, and treat the winds and waves as things subject to the power of faith, and therefore to be commanded into quiet. We shall speak so as to console others : our calm shall work marvels in the little ships whereof others are captains. We, too, shall say, " Peace ! Be still." Our confidence shall prove contagious, and the timid shall grow brave : our tender love shall spread itself, and the contentious shall cool down to patience. Only the matter must begin within ourselves. We cannot create a calm till we are in a calm. It is easier to rule the elements than to govern the unruliness of our wayward nature. When grace has made us masters of our fears, so that we can take a pillow and fall asleep amid the hurricane, the fury of the tempest is over. He giveth peace and safety when He giveth His beloved sleep.

" And Jesus said, Somebody hath touched Me: for I perceive that virtue is gone out of Me."—*Luke* viii. 46.

4

Real Contact with Jesus

OUR Lord was very frequently in the midst of a
crowd. His preaching was so plain and so
forcible that He always attracted a vast company of
hearers ; and, moreover, the rumour of the loaves and
fishes no doubt had something to do with increasing
His audiences, while the expectation of beholding a
miracle would be sure to add to the numbers of the
hangers-on. Our Lord Jesus Christ often found it
difficult to move through the streets, because of the
masses who pressed upon Him. This was encourag-
ing to Him as a preacher, and yet how small a
residuum of real good came of all the excitement
which gathered around His personal ministry! He
might have looked upon the great mass, and have
said, " What is the chaff to the wheat ? " for here it
was piled up upon the threshing-floor, heap upon
heap ; and yet, after His decease, His disciples might
have been counted by a few scores, for those who had
spiritually received Him were but few. Many were
called, but few were chosen. Yet, wherever one was
blessed, our Saviour took note of it ; it touched a
chord in His soul. He never could be unaware when
virtue had gone out of Him to heal a sick one, or
when power had gone forth with His ministry to save
a sinful one. Of all the crowd that gathered round
the Saviour upon the day of which our text speaks,

I find nothing said about one of them except this solitary "somebody" who had touched Him. The crowd came, and the crowd went ; but little is recorded of it all. Just as the ocean, having advanced to full tide, leaves but little behind it when it retires again to its channel, so the vast multitude around the Saviour left only this one precious deposit—one "somebody" who had touched Him, and had received virtue from Him.

Ah, my Master, it may be so again this evening! These Sabbath mornings, and these Sabbath evenings, the crowds come pouring in like a mighty ocean, filling this house, and then they all retire again ; only here and there is a "somebody" left weeping for sin, a "somebody" left rejoicing in Christ, a "somebody" who can say, "I have touched the hem of His garment, and I have been made whole." The whole of my other hearers are not worth the "somebodies." The many of you are not worth the few, for the many are the pebbles, and the few are the diamonds ; the many are the heaps of husks, and the few are the precious grains. May God find them out at this hour, and His shall be all the praise!

Jesus said, "Somebody hath touched Me," from which we observe that, *in the use of means and ordinances, we should never be satisfied unless we get into personal contact with Christ*, so that we touch Him, as this woman touched His garment. Secondly, *if we can get into such personal contact, we shall have a blessing:* "I perceive that virtue is gone out of Me ;" and, thirdly, *if we do get a blessing, Christ will know it ;* however obscure our case may be, He will know it, and He will have us let others know it ; He will

54

speak, and ask such questions as will draw us out, and manifest us to the world.

I. First, then, IN THE USE OF ALL MEANS AND ORDINANCES, LET IT BE OUR CHIEF AIM AND OBJECT TO COME INTO PERSONAL CONTACT WITH THE LORD JESUS CHRIST.

Peter said, " The multitude throng Thee, and press Thee," and that is true of the multitude to this very day ; but of those who come where Christ is in the assembly of His saints, a large proportion only come because it is their custom to do so. Perhaps they hardly know why they go to a place of worship. They go because they always did go, and they think it wrong not to go. They are just like the doors which swing upon their hinges ; they take no interest in what is done, at least only in the exterior parts of the service ; into the heart and soul of the business they do not enter, and cannot enter. They are glad if the sermon is rather short, there is so much the less tedium for them. They are glad if they can look around and gaze at the congregation, they find in that something to interest them ; but getting near to the Lord Jesus is not the business they come upon. They have not looked at it in that light. They come and they go ; they come and they go ; and it will be so till, by-and-by, they will come for the last time, and they will find out in the next world that the means of grace were not instituted to be matters of custom, and that to have heard Jesus Christ preached, and to have rejected Him, is no trifle, but a solemn thing for which they will have to answer in the presence of the great Judge of all the earth.

Others there are who come to the house of prayer,

and try to enter into the service, and do so in a certain fashion; but it is only self-righteously or professionally. They may come to the Lord's table; perhaps they attend to baptism; they may even join the church. They are baptized, yet not by the Holy Spirit; they take the Lord's supper, but they take not the Lord Himself; they eat the bread, but they never eat His flesh; they drink the wine, but they never drink His blood; they have been buried in the pool, but they have never been buried with Christ in baptism, nor have they risen again with Him into newness of life. To them, to read, to sing, to kneel, to hear, and so on, are enough. They are content with the shell, but the blessed spiritual kernel, the true marrow and fatness, these they know nothing of. These are the many, go into what church or meeting-house you please. They are in the press around Jesus, but they do not touch Him. They come, but they come not into contact with Jesus. They are outward, external hearers only, but there is no inward touching of the blessed person of Christ, no mysterious contact with the ever-blessed Saviour, no stream of life and love flowing from Him to them. It is all mechanical religion. Of vital godliness, they know nothing.

But, "somebody," said Christ, "somebody hath touched Me," and that is the soul of the matter. O my hearer, when you are in prayer alone, never be satisfied with having prayed; do not give it up till you have touched Christ in prayer; or, if you have not got to Him, at any rate sigh and cry until you do! Do not think you have prayed, but try again. When you come to public worship, I beseech you, rest not satisfied with listening to the sermon, and so on,—as you all do with sufficient attention ; to that I bear you witness ;—but do not be content unless you get at Christ the Master, and touch Him. At all times when you come to the communion table, count it to have been no ordinance of grace to you unless you have gone right through the veil into Christ's own arms, or at least have touched His garment, feeling that the first object, the life and soul of the means of grace, is to touch Jesus Christ Himself; and except "somebody" hath touched Him, the whole has been a mere dead performance, without life or power.

The woman in our text was not only amongst those who were in the crowd, but she touched Jesus ; and therefore, beloved, let me hold her up to your example in some respects, though I would to God that in other respects you might excel her.

Note, first, she felt that it was of no use being in the crowd, of no use to be in the same street with Christ, or near to the place where Christ was, but *she must get at Him ; she must touch Him.* She touched Him, you will notice, under *many difficulties.* There was a great crowd. She was a woman. She was also a woman enfeebled by a long disease which had drained her constitution, and left her more fit to be upon a bed than to be struggling in the seething tumult. Yet, notwithstanding that, so intense was her desire, that she urged on her way, I doubt not with many a bruise, and many an uncouth push, and at last, poor trembler as she was, she got near to the Lord. Beloved, it is not always easy to get at Jesus. It is very easy to kneel down to pray, but not so easy to reach Christ in prayer. There is a child crying, it is your own, and its noise has often hindered you when you were striving to approach Jesus; or a knock will come at the door when you most wish to be retired. When you are sitting in the house of God, your neighbour in the seat before you may unconsciously distract your attention. It is not easy to draw near to Christ, especially coming as some of you do right away from the counting-house, and from the workshop, with a thousand thoughts and cares about you. You cannot always unload your burden outside, and come in here with your hearts prepared to receive the gospel. Ah! it is a terrible fight sometimes, a real foot-to-foot fight with evil, with temptation, and I know not what. But, beloved, do fight it out, do fight it out; do not let your seasons for prayer be wasted, nor your times for hearing be thrown away; but, like this woman, be resolved, with all your feebleness, that you will lay hold upon Christ. And oh! if you be resolved about it, if you cannot get to Him, He will come to you, and sometimes, when you are struggling against unbelieving thoughts, He will turn and say, "Make room for that poor feeble one, that she may come to Me, for My desire is to the work of My own hands; let her come to Me, and let her desire be granted to her."

Observe, again, that this woman touched Jesus *very secretly*. Perhaps there is a dear sister here who is getting near to Christ at this very moment, and yet her face does not betray her. It is so little contact that she has gained with Christ that the joyous flush, and the sparkle of the eye, which we often see in the child of God, have not yet come to her. She is sitting in yonder obscure corner, or standing in this aisle, but though her touch is secret, it is true. Though she cannot tell another of it, yet it is accomplished. She has touched Jesus. Beloved, that is not always the nearest fellowship with Christ of which we talk the most. Deep waters are still. Nay, I am not sure but what we sometimes get nearer to Christ when we think we are at a distance than we do when we imagine we are near Him, for we are not always exactly the best judges of our own spiritual state, and we may be very close to the Master, and yet for all that we may be so anxious to get closer that we may feel dissatisfied with the measure of grace which we have already received. To be satisfied with self, is no sign of grace; but to long for more grace, is often a far better evidence of the healthy state of the soul. Friend, if thou canst not come to the table to-night publicly, come to the Master in secret. If thou darest not tell thy wife, or thy child, or thy father, that thou art trusting in Jesus, it need not be told as yet. Thou mayest do it secretly, as he did to whom Jesus said, "When thou wast under the fig tree, I saw thee." Nathanael retired to the shade that no one might see him; but Jesus saw him, and marked his prayer, and He will see thee in the crowd, and in the dark, and not withhold His blessing.

This woman also came into contact with Christ *under a very deep sense of unworthiness.* I dare say she thought, "If I touch the Great Prophet, it will be a wonder if He does not strike me with some sudden judgment," for she was a woman ceremonially unclean. She had no right to be in the throng. Had the Levitical law been strictly carried out, I suppose she would have been confined to her house; but there she was wandering about, and she must needs go and touch the holy Saviour. Ah! poor heart, you feel to-night that you are not fit to touch the skirts of the Master's robe, for you are so unworthy. You never felt so undeserving before as you do to-night. In the recollection of last week and its infirmities, in the remembrance of the present state of your heart, and all its wanderings from God, you feel as if there never was so worthless a sinner in the house of God before. "Is grace for me?" say you. "Is Christ for me?" Oh! yes, unworthy one. Do not be put off without it. Jesus Christ does not save the worthy, but the unworthy. Your plea must not be righteousness, but guilt. And you, too, child of God, though you are ashamed of yourself, Jesus is not ashamed of you; and though you feel unfit to come, let your unfitness only impel you with the greater earnestness of desire. Let your sense of need make you the more fervent to approach the Lord, who can supply your need.

Thus, you see, the woman came under difficulties, she came secretly, she came as an unworthy one, but still she obtained the blessing.

I have known many staggered with that saying of Paul's, "He that eateth and drinketh unworthily, eateth and drinketh damnation to himself." Now, understand that this passage does not refer to the unworthiness of those persons who come to the Lord's table; for it does not say, "He that eateth and drinketh *being unworthy*." It is not an adjective; it is an adverb: "He that eateth and drinketh un-worth*ily*," that is to say, he who shall come to the outward and visible sign of Christ's presence, and shall eat of the bread in order to obtain money by being a member of the church, knowing himself to be a hypocrite, or who shall do it jestingly, trifling with the ordinance : such a person would be eating and drinking unworthily, and he will be condemned. The sense of the passage is, not "damnation", as our version reads it, but "condemnation." There can be no doubt that members of the church, coming to the Lord's table in an unworthy manner, do receive condemnation. They are condemned for so doing, and the Lord is grieved. If they have any conscience at all, they ought to feel their sin ; and if not, they may expect the chastisements of God to visit them. But, O sinner, as to coming to Christ,—which is a very different thing from coming to the Lord's table,—as to coming to Christ, the more unworthy you feel yourself to be, the better. Come, thou filthy one, for Christ can wash thee. Come, thou loathsome one, for Christ can beautify thee. Come utterly ruined and undone, for in Jesus Christ there is the strength and salvation which thy case requires.

Notice, once again, that *this woman touched the Master very tremblingly, and it was only a hurried touch, but still it was the touch of faith*. Oh, beloved, to lay hold on Christ ! Be thankful if you do but get near Him for a few minutes. "Abide with me," should be your prayer ; but oh, if He only give you a glimpse, be thankful ! Remember that a touch healed the woman. She did not embrace Christ by the hour together. She had but a touch, and she was healed ; and oh, may you have a sight of Jesus now, my beloved ! Though it be but a glimpse, yet it will gladden and cheer your souls. Perhaps you are waiting on Christ, desiring His company, and while

you are turning it over in your mind you are asking,
"Will He ever shine upon me? Will He ever speak
loving words to me? Will He ever let me sit at His
feet? Will He ever permit me to lean my head
upon His bosom?" Come and try Him. Though
you should shake like an aspen leaf, yet come. They
sometimes come best who come most tremblingly, for
when the creature is lowest then is the Creator highest,
and when in our own esteem we are less than nothing
and vanity, then is Christ the more fair and lovely in
our eyes. One of the best ways of climbing to heaven
is on our hands and knees. At any rate, there is no
fear of falling when we are in that position, for—

"He that is down need fear no fall."

Let your lowliness of heart, your sense of utter
nothingness, instead of disqualifying you, be a sweet
medium for leading you to receive more of Christ.
The more empty I am, the more room is there for my
Master. The more I lack, the more He will give me.
The more I feel my sickness, the more shall I adore
and bless Him when He makes me whole.

You see, the woman did really touch Christ, and so
I come back to that. Whatever infirmity there was
in the touch, it was a real touch of faith. She did
reach Christ Himself. She did not touch Peter ; that
would have been of no use to her, any more than it is
for the parish priest to tell you that you are regenerate
when your life soon proves that you are not. She did
not touch John or James ; that would have been of
no more good to her than it is for you to be touched
by a bishop's hands, and to be told that you are confirmed in the faith, when you are not even a believer,

and therefore have no faith to be confirmed in. She touched the Master Himself; and, I pray you, do not be content unless you can do the same. Put out the hand of faith, and touch Christ. Rest on Him. Rely on His bloody sacrifice, His dying love, His rising power, His ascended plea; and as you rest in Him, your vital touch, however feeble, will certainly give you the blessing your soul needs.

This brings us to the second part of our discourse, upon which I will say only a little.

II. THE WOMAN IN THE CROWD DID TOUCH JESUS, AND, HAVING DONE SO, SHE RECEIVED VIRTUE FROM HIM.

The healing energy streamed at once through the finger of faith into the woman. In Christ, there is healing for all spiritual diseases. There is a speedy healing, a healing which will not take months nor years, but which is complete in one second. There is in Christ a sufficient healing, though your diseases should be multiplied beyond all bounds. There is in Christ an all-conquering power to drive out every ill. Though, like this woman, you baffle physicians, and your case is reckoned desperate beyond all parallel, yet a touch of Christ will heal you. What a precious, glorious gospel I have to preach to sinners! If they touch Jesus, no matter though the devil himself were in them, that touch of faith would drive the devil out of them. Though you were like the man into whom there had entered a legion of devils, the word of Jesus would cast them all into the deep, and you should sit at His feet, clothed, and in your right mind. There is no excess or extravagance of sin which the power of Jesus Christ cannot overcome. If thou canst believe, whatever thou mayest have been, thou shalt be saved. If thou canst believe, though thou hast been lying in the scarlet dye till the warp and woof of thy being are ingrained therewith, yet shall the precious blood of Jesus make thee white as snow. Though thou art become black as hell itself, and only fit to be cast into the pit, yet if thou trustest Jesus, that simple faith shall give to thy soul the healing which shall make thee fit to tread the streets of heaven, and to stand before Jehovah-Rophi's face, magnifying the Lord that healeth thee.

And now, child of God, I want you to learn the same lesson. Very likely, when you came in here, you said,—" Alas! I feel very dull; my spirituality is at a very low ebb; the place is hot, and I do not feel prepared to hear; the spirit is willing, but the flesh is weak; I shall have no holy enjoyment to-day!" Why not? Why, the touch of Jesus could make you live if you were dead, and surely it will stir the life that is in you, though it may seem to you to be expiring! Now, struggle hard, my beloved, to get at Jesus! May the Eternal Spirit come and help you, and may you yet find that your dull, dead times can soon become your best times. Oh! what a blessing it is that God takes the beggar up from the dunghill! He does not raise us when He sees us already up, but when He finds us lying on the dunghill, then He delights to lift us up, and set us among princes. Or ever you are aware, your soul may become like the chariots of Ammi-nadib. Up from the depths of heaviness to the very heights of ecstatic worship you may mount as in a single moment if you can but touch Christ crucified. View Him yonder, with streaming wounds, with thorn-crowned head, as in all the majesty of His misery, He expires for you!

"Alas!" say you, "I have a thousand doubts to-night." Ah! but your doubts will soon vanish when you draw nigh to Christ. He never doubts who feels the touch of Christ, at least, not while the touch lasts, for observe this woman! She felt in her body that she was made whole, and so shall you, if you will only come into contact with the Lord. Do not wait for evidences, but come to Christ for evidences. If you cannot even dream of a good thing in yourselves, come to Jesus Christ as you did at the first. Come as if you never had come at all. Come to Jesus as a sinner, and your doubts shall flee away.

"Ay!" saith another, "but my sins come to my remembrance, my sins since conversion." Well, return to Jesus, when your guilt seems to return. The fountain is still open, and that fountain, you will remember, is not only open for sinners, but for saints ; for what saith the Scripture—" There shall be a fountain opened *for the house of David and for the inhabitants of Jerusalem*,"—that is, for you, church-members, for you, believers in Jesus? The fountain is still open. Come, beloved, come to Jesus anew, and whatever be your sins, or doubts, or heaviness, they shall all depart as soon as you can touch your Lord.

III. And now the last point is—and I will not detain you long upon it — IF SOMEBODY SHALL TOUCH JESUS, THE LORD WILL KNOW IT.

I do not know your names ; a great number of you are perfect strangers to me. It matters nothing ; your name is "somebody", and Christ will know you. You are a total stranger, perhaps, to everybody in

65

this place ; but if you get a blessing, there will be two who will know it,—you will, and Christ will. Oh! if you should look to Jesus this day, it may not be registered in our church-book, and we may not hear of it ; but ·still it will be registered in the courts of heaven, and they will set all the bells of the New Jerusalem a-ringing, and all the harps of angels will take a fresh lease of music as soon as they know that you are born again.

> " With joy the Father doth approve
>   The fruit of His eternal love ;
> The Son with joy looks down and sees
>   The purchase of His agonies ;
> The Spirit takes delight to view
>   The holy soul He formed anew ;
> And saints and angels join to sing
>   The growing empire of their King."

" Somebody !" I do not know the woman's name ; I do not know who the man is, but—" Somebody !"— God's electing love rests on thee, Christ's redeeming blood was shed for thee, the Spirit has wrought a work in thee, or thou wouldst not have touched Jesus ; and all this Jesus knows.

It is a consoling thought that Christ not only knows the great children in the family, but He also knows the little ones. This stands fast : " The Lord knoweth them that are His," whether they are only brought to know Him now, or whether they have known Him for fifty years. " The Lord knoweth them that are His," and if I am a part of Christ's body, I may be but the foot, but the Lord knows the foot ; and the head and the heart in heaven feel acutely when the foot on earth is bruised. If you have touched Jesus, I tell you that amidst the glories of angels, and the everlasting hallelujahs of all the blood-bought, He has found time to hear your sigh, to receive your faith, and to give you an answer of peace. All the way from heaven to earth there has rushed a mighty stream of healing virtue, which has come from Christ to you. Since you have touched Him, the healing virtue has touched you.

Now, *as Jesus knows of your salvation, He wishes other people to know of it*, and that is why He has put it into my heart to say,—Somebody has touched the Lord. Where is that somebody ? Somebody, where are you ? Somebody, where are you ? You have touched Christ, though with a feeble finger, and you are saved. Let us know it. It is due to us to let us know. You cannot guess what joy it gives us when we hear of sick ones being healed by our Master. Some of you, perhaps, have known the Lord for months, and you have not yet come forward to make an avowal of it ; we beg you to do so. You may come forward tremblingly, as this woman did ; you may perhaps say, " I do not know what I should tell you." Well, you must tell us what she told the Lord ; she told Him all the truth. We do not want anything else. We do not desire any sham experience. We do not want you to manufacture feelings like somebody else's that you have read of in a book. Come and tell us what you have felt. We shall not ask you to tell us what you have not felt, or what you do not know. But, if you have touched Christ, and you have been healed, I ask it, and I think I may ask it as your duty, as well as a favour to us, to come and tell us what the Lord hath done for your soul.

And you, believers, when you come to the Lord's table, if you draw near to Christ, and have a sweet season, tell it to your brethren. Just as when Benjamin's brethren went down to Egypt to buy corn, they left Benjamin at home, but they took a sack for Benjamin, so you ought always to take a word home for the sick wife at home, or the child who cannot come out. Take home food for those of the family who cannot come for it. God grant that you may have always something sweet to tell of what you have experimentally known of precious truth, for while the sermon may have been sweet in itself, it comes with a double power when you can add, " and there was a savour about it which I enjoyed, and which made my heart leap for joy " !

Whoever you may be, my dear friend, though you may be nothing but a poor " somebody ", yet if you have touched Christ, tell others about it, in order that they may come and touch Him, too ; and the Lord bless you, for Christ's sake ! Amen.

" Behold, My Servant shall deal prudently, He shall be exalted and extolled, and be very high. As many were astonied at Thee; His visage was so marred more than any man, and His form more than the sons of men; so shall He sprinkle many nations; the kings shall shut their mouths at Him: for that which had not been told them shall they see; and that which they had not heard shall they consider."

Isaiah lii. 13—15

5

Jesus, the Great Object of Astonishment

OUR Lord Jesus Christ bore from of old the name of "WONDERFUL", and the word seems all too poor to set forth His marvellous person and character. He says of Himself, in the language of the prophet,—"Behold, I and the children whom the Lord hath given Me are for signs and for wonders." He is a fountain of astonishment to all who know Him. and the more they know of Him, the more are they "astonied" at Him. It is an astonishing thing that there should have been a Christ at all: the Incarnation is the miracle of miracles ; that He who is the Infinite should become an infant, that He who made the worlds should be wrapt in swaddling-bands, remains a fact out of which, as from a hive, new wonders continually fly forth. In His complex nature He is so mysterious, and yet so manifest, that doubtless all the angels of heaven were and are astonished at Him. O Son of God, and Son of man, when Thou, the Word, wast made flesh, and dwelt among us, and Thy saints beheld Thy glory, it was but natural that many should be astonished at Thee !

Our text seems to say that our Lord was, first, *a great wonder in His griefs;* and, secondly, that He was *a great wonder in His glory.*

I. HE WAS A GREAT WONDER IN HIS GRIEFS : "As many were astonied at Thee ; His visage was so marred more than any man, and His form more than the sons of men."

His visage was marred : no doubt His countenance bore the signs of a matchless grief. There were ploughings on His brow as well as upon His back ; suffering, and brokenness of spirit, and agony of heart, had told upon that lovely face, till its beauty, though never to be destroyed, was " so " marred that never was any other so spoiled with sorrow. But it was not His face only, His whole form was marred more than the sons of men. The contour of His bodily manhood showed marks of singular assaults of sorrow, such as had never bowed another form so low. I do not know whether His gait was stooping, or whether His knees tottered, and His walk was feeble ; but there was evidently a something about Him which gave Him the appearance of premature age, since to the Jews He looked older than He was, for when He was little more than thirty they said unto Him, " Thou art not yet fifty years old." I cannot conceive that He was deformed or ungainly ; but despite His natural dignity, His worn and emaciated appearance marked Him out as "the Man of sorrows", and to the carnal eye His whole natural and spiritual form had in it nothing which evoked admiration ; even as the prophet said, " When we shall see Him, there is no beauty that we should desire Him." The marring was not of that lovely face alone, but of the whole fabric of His wondrous manhood, so that many were astonied at Him.

Our astonishment, when in contemplation we behold our suffering Lord, will arise from the consideration of what His natural beauty must have been, enshrined as He was from the first within a perfect body. Conceived without sin, and so born of a pure virgin without taint of hereditary sin, I doubt not that He was the flower and glory of manhood as to His form, and from His early youth He must have been a joy to His mother's eye. Great masters of the olden time expended all their skill upon the holy child Jesus, but it is not for the colours of earth to depict the Lord from heaven. That "holy thing" which was born of Mary was "seen of angels," and it charmed their eyes. Must such loveliness be marred? His every look was pure, His every thought was holy, and therefore the expression of His face must have been heavenly, and yet it must be marred. Poverty must mark it; hunger, and thirst, and weariness, must plough it; heart-griefs must seam and scar it; spittle must distain it; tears must scald it; smiting must bruise it; death must make it pale and bloodless. Well does Bernard sing,—

> "O sacred Head, once wounded,
>   With grief and pain weigh'd down,
> How scornfully surrounded
>   With thorns, Thine only crown;
> How pale art Thou with anguish,
>   With sore abuse and scorn!
> How does that visage languish,
>   Which once was bright as morn!"

The second astonishment to us must be that he could be so marred who had nothing in His character to mar His countenance. Sin is a sad disfigurement to faces which in early childhood were surpassingly attractive. Passion, if it be indulged in, soon sets a seal of deformity upon the countenance. Men that

73

plunge into vice bear upon their features the traces of their hearts' volcanic fires. We most of us know some withered beings, whose beauty has been burned up by the fierce fires of excess, till they are a horror to look upon, as if the mark of Cain were set upon them. Every sin makes its line on a fair face. But there was no sin in the blessed Jesus, no evil thought to mar His natural perfectness. No redness of eyes ever came to Him by tarrying long at the wine; no unhallowed anger ever flushed His cheek; no covetousness gave to His eye a wolfish glance; no selfish care lent to His features a sharp and anxious cast. Such an unselfish, holy life as His ought to have rendered Him, if it had been possible, more beautiful every day. Indulging such benevolence, abiding in such communion with God, surely the face of Christ must, in the natural order of things, have more and more astonished all sympathetic observers with its transcendent charms. But sorrow came to engrave her name where sin had never made a stroke, and she did her work so effectually that His visage was more marred than that of any man, although the God of mercy knows there have been other visages that have been worn with pain and anguish past all recognition. I need not repeat even one of the many stories of human woe : that of our Lord surpasses all.

Remember that the face of our Well-beloved, as well as all His form, must have been an accurate index of His soul. Physiognomy is a science with much truth in it when it deals with men of truth. Men weaned from simplicity know how to control their countenances; the crafty will appear to be honest, the hardened will seem to sympathize with the distressed, the revengeful will mimic good-will. There are some who continually use their countenance as they do their speech, to conceal their feelings ; and it is almost a point of politeness with them never to show themselves, but always to go masked among their fellows.

But the Christ had learned no such arts. He was so sincere, so transparent, so child-like and true, that whatever stirred within Him was apparent to those about Him, so far as they were capable of understanding His great soul. We read of Him that He was "moved with compassion." The Greek word means that He experienced a wonderful emotion of His whole nature, He was thrilled with it, and His disciples saw how deeply He felt for the people, who were as sheep without a shepherd. Though He did not commit Himself to men, He did not conceal Himself, but wore His heart upon His sleeve, and all could see what He was, and knew that He was full of grace and truth. We are, therefore, not surprised, when we devoutly consider our Lord's character, that His visage and form should indicate the inward agonies of His tender spirit ; it could not be that His face should be untrue to His heart. The ploughers made deep furrows upon His soul as well as upon His back, and His heart was rent with inward convulsions, which could not but affect His whole appearance. Those eyes saw what those around Him could not see; those shoulders bore a constant burden which others could not know ; and, therefore, His countenance and form betrayed the fact. O dear, dear Saviour, when we think of Thee, and of Thy majesty and purity, we are again astonished that woes should come upon Thee so grievously as to mar Thy visage and Thy form !

Now think, dear friends, what were the causes of this marring. It was not old age that had wrinkled His brow, for He was still in the prime of life, neither was it a personal sickness which had caused decay ; much less was it any congenital weakness and disease, which at length betrayed itself, for in His flesh there was no possibility of impurity, which would, in death, have led to corruption. It was occasioned, first, by His constant sympathy with the suffering. There was a heavy wear and tear occasioned by the extra-ordinary compassion of His soul. In three years it had told upon Him most manifestly, till His visage was marred more than that of any other man. To Him there was a kind of sucking up into Himself of all the suffering of those whom He blessed. He always bore upon Him the burden of mortal woe. We read of Christ healing all that were sick, " that it might be fulfilled which was spoken by Esaias the prophet, saying, Himself took our infirmities, and bare our sicknesses." Yes, He took those infirmities and sicknesses in some mystical way to Himself, just as I have heard of certain trees, which scatter health, because they themselves imbibe the miasma, and draw up into themselves those noxious vapours which other-wise would poison mankind. Thus, without being themselves polluted, they disinfect the atmosphere around them. This, our Saviour did, but the cost was great to Him. You can imagine, living as He did in the midst of one vast hospital, how constantly He must have seen sights that grieved and pained Him. Moreover, with a nature so pure and loving, He must have been daily tortured with the sin, and hypocrisy, and oppression which so abounded in His day. In a certain sense, He was always laying down His life for men, for He was spent in their service, tortured by their sin, and oppressed with their sorrow. The more we look into that marred visage, the more shall we be astonished at the anguish which it indicated.

Do not wonder that He was more marred than any man, for He was more sensitive than other men. No part of Him was callous, He had no seared conscience, no blunted sensibility, no drugged and deadened nerve. His manhood was in its glory, in the perfection in which Adam was when God made him in His own image, and therefore He was ill-housed in such a fallen world. We read of Christ that He was "grieved for the hardness of their hearts," "He marvelled because of their unbelief," "He sighed deeply in His spirit," "He groaned in the spirit, and was troubled." This, however, was only the beginning of the marring.

His deepest griefs and most grievous marring came of *His substitutionary work*, while bearing the penalty of our sin. One word recalls much of His woe: it is, "Gethsemane." Betrayed by Judas, His trusted friend, that the Scripture might be fulfilled, "He that eateth bread with Me hath lifted up his heel against Me;" deserted even by John, for all the disciples forsook Him and fled; not one of all the loved ones with Him: He was left alone. He had washed their feet, but they could not watch with Him one hour; and in that garden He wrestled with our deadly foe, till His sweat was as it were great drops of blood falling down to the ground, and as Hart puts it, He—

> "Bore all Incarnate God could bear,
> With strength enough, but none to spare."

I do verily believe that verse to be true. Herein you see what marred His countenance, and His form, even while in life. The whole of His manhood felt that dreadful shock, when He and the prince of darkness, in awful duel, fought it out amidst the gloom of the olives on that cold midnight when our redemption began to be fully accomplished.

The whole of His passion marred His countenance and His form with its unknown sufferings. I restrain myself, lest this meditation should grow too painful. They bound Him, they scourged Him, they mocked Him, they plucked off the hair from His face, they spat upon Him, and at last they nailed Him to the tree, and there He hung. His physical pain alone must have been very great, but all the while there was within His soul an inward torment which added immeasurably to His sufferings. His God forsook Him. "Eloi, Eloi, lama, sabachthani?" is a voice enough to rend the rocks, and assuredly it makes us all astonished when, in the returning light, we look upon His visage, and are sure that never face of any man was so marred before, and never form of any son of man so grievously disfigured. Weeping and wondering, astonied and adoring, we leave the griefs of our own dear Lord, and with loving interest turn to the brighter portion of His unrivalled story.

> "Behold your King! Though the moonlight steals
>   Through the silvery sprays of the olive tree,
> No star-gemmed sceptre or crown it reveals,
>   In the solemn shade of Gethsemane.
>   Only a form of prostrate grief,
>   Fallen, crushed, like a broken leaf!
> Oh, think of His sorrow, that we may know
> The depth of love in the depth of woe!

"Behold your King, with His sorrow crowned,
Alone, alone in the valley is He!
The shadows of death are gathering round,
And the cross must follow Gethsemane.
Darker and darker the gloom must fall,
Filled is the cup, He must drink it all!
Oh, think of His sorrow, that we may know
His wondrous love in His wondrous woe!"

II. There is AN EQUAL ASTONISHMENT AT HIS GLORIES. I doubt not, if we could see Him now, as He appeared to John in Patmos, we should feel that we must do exactly as the beloved disciple did, for He deliberately wrote, " When I saw Him, I fell at His feet as dead." His astonishment was so great that he could not endure the sight. He had doubtless longed often to behold that glorified face and form, but the privilege was too much for him. While we are encumbered with these frail bodies, it is not fit for us to behold our Lord, for we should die with excess of delight if we were suddenly to behold that vision of splendour. Oh, for those glorious days when we shall lie for ever at His feet, and see our exalted Lord!

"Behold, My servant shall deal prudently, He shall be exalted and extolled, and be very high." Observe the three words, " exalted and extolled, and be very high;" language pants for expression. Our Lord is now *exalted* in being lifted up from the grave, lifted up above all angels, and principalities, and powers. The Man Christ Jesus is the nearest to the eternal throne, ay, the Lamb is before the throne. "And I beheld, and, lo, in the midst of the throne and of the four beasts, and in the midst of the elders, stood a Lamb as it had been slain." He is in His own state

and person exalted, and then by the praise rendered Him he is *extolled*, for he is worshipped and adored by the whole universe. All praise goes up before Him now, so that men extol Him, while "God also hath highly exalted Him, and given Him a name, which is above every name ; that at the name of Jesus every knee should bow, of things in heaven, and things in earth, and things under the earth ; and that every tongue should confess that Jesus Christ is Lord, to the glory of God the Father." Deep were His sorrows, but as high are His joys. It is said that, around many of the lochs in Scotland, the mountains are as high as the water is deep ; and so our Lord's glories are as immeasurable as were His woes. What a meditation is furnished by these two-fold and incalculable heights and depths ! Our text says that He shall "*be very high*." It cannot tell us how high. It is inconceivable how great and glorious in all respects the Lord Jesus Christ is at this moment. Oh, that He may be very high in our esteem ! He is not yet exalted and extolled in any of our hearts as He deserves to be. I would we loved Him a thousand times as much as we do, but our whole heart goeth after Him, does it not ? Would we not die for Him ? Would we not set Him on a throne as high as seven heavens, and then think that we had not done enough for Him, who is now our all in all, and more than all ?

You notice what is said, concerning the Christ, as the most astonishing thing of all : "*So shall He sprinkle many nations.*" Now is it the glory of our risen Lord, at this moment, that His precious blood is to save many nations. Before the throne, men of all nations shall sing, "Thou wast slain, and hast redeemed us unto God by Thy blood." Not the English nation alone shall be purified by His atoning blood, but many nations shall He sprinkle with His reconciling blood, even as Israel of old was sprinkled with the blood of sacrifice. We read in the tenth chapter of the Epistle to the Hebrews, at the twenty-second verse, of "having our hearts sprinkled from an evil conscience," and this is effected by that precious blood by which we have been once purged so effectually that we have no more consciousness of sins, but enter into perfect peace. The blood of bulls and of goats, and the ashes of an heifer, sprinkling the unclean, sanctified to the purifying of the flesh, and much more doth the blood of Christ purge our conscience from dead works, to serve the living God.

The sprinkling of the blood was meant also to confirm the covenant : thus Moses "sprinkled both the book and all the people, saying, This is the blood of the testament which God hath enjoined unto you." Our Lord Himself said, " This is My blood of the new covenant, which is shed for many for the remission of sins." But is it not a wonderful thing that He should die as a malefactor on the tree, amid scorn and ridicule, and yet that He is this day bringing nations into covenant with God ? Once so despised, and now so mighty ! God has given Him " for a covenant of the people, for a light of the Gentiles." Many nations shall by Him be joined in covenant with the God of the whole earth. Do not fall into the erroneous idea that this world is like a great ship-wrecked vessel, soon to go to pieces on an iron-bound coast ; but rather let us expect the conversion of the world to the

Lord Jesus. As a reward for the travail of His soul, He shall cause many nations to " exult with joy ", for so some read the passage ; the peoples of the earth shall not only be astonished at His griefs, but they shall admire His glories, adore His perfections, and be filled with an amazement of joy at His coming and kingdom. I can conceive nothing in the future too great and glorious to result from the passion and death of our Divine Lord.

Listen to this, "*Kings shall shut their mouths at Him.*" They shall see such a King as they themselves have never been ; they speak freely to their brother-kings, but they shall not dare to speak to Him, and as for speaking against Him, that will be altogether out of the question.

> " Kings shall fall down before Him,
> And gold and incense bring."

" *For that which had not been told them shall they see.*" Kings are often out of the reach of the gospel, they do not hear it, it is not told to them. They would despise the lowly preacher, and little gatherings of believers meeting together for worship ; they would only listen to stately discourses, which do not touch the heart and conscience. The great ones of the earth are usually the least likely to know the things of God, for while the poor have the gospel preached unto them, princes are more likely to hear soft flatteries and fair speeches. The time shall come, however, when Cæsar shall bow before a real Imperator, and monarchs shall behold the Prince of the kings of the earth. " For the Lord Himself shall descend from heaven with a shout, with the voice of the archangel, and with the trump of God." They shall see His majesty, of which they had not even been told.

"*That which they had not heard shall they consider.*" They shall be obliged, even on their thrones, to think about the kingdom of the King of kings, and they shall retire to their closets to confess their sins, and to put on sackcloth and ashes, and to give heed to the words of wisdom. "Be wise now, therefore, O ye kings : be instructed, ye judges of the earth." To-day, the humble listen to Christ, but by-and-by the mightiest of the mighty shall turn all their thoughts towards Him. He shall gather sheaves of sceptres beneath His arm, and crowns shall be strewn at His feet ; and "He shall reign for ever and ever," and "of the increase of His government and peace there shall be no end." If we were astonished at the marring of His face, we shall be much more astonished at the magnificence of His glory. Upon His throne none shall question His supremacy, none shall doubt His loveliness ; but His enemies shall weep and wail because of Him whom they pierced ; while He shall be admired in all them that believe. Adorable Lord, we long for Thy glorious appearing ! We beseech Thee. tarry not !

> " Come, and begin Thy reign
>   Of everlasting peace ;
>   Come, take the kingdom to Thyself,
>   Great King of Righteousness ! "

" Who His own self bare our sins in His own body on the tree, that we, being dead to sins, should live unto righteousness : by whose stripes ye were healed. For ye were as sheep going astray ; but are now returned unto the Shepherd and Bishop of your souls."—1 *Peter* ii. 24, 25.

6

The Sin-Bearer

THIS wonderful passage is a part of Peter's address to servants; and in his day nearly all servants were slaves. Peter begins at the eighteenth verse : " Servants, be subject to your masters with all fear ; not only to the good and gentle, but also to the froward. For this is thankworthy, if a man for conscience toward God endure grief, suffering wrongfully. For what glory is it, if, when ye be buffeted for your faults, ye shall take it patiently? but if, when ye do well, and suffer for it, ye take it patiently, this is acceptable with God. For even hereunto were ye called : because Christ also suffered for us, leaving us an example, that ye should follow His steps : who did no sin, neither was guile found in His mouth : who, when He was reviled, reviled not again ; when He suffered, He threatened not ; but committed Himself to Him that judgeth righteously : who His own self bare our sins in His own body on the tree, that we, being dead to sins, should live unto righteousness : by whose stripes ye were healed." If we are in a lowly condition of life, we shall find our best comfort in thinking of the lowly Saviour bearing our sins in all patience and submission. If we are called to suffer, as servants often were in the Roman times, we shall be solaced by a vision of our Lord buffeted, scourged, and crucified, yet silent in the majesty of His endurance. If these sufferings are entirely undeserved, and we are grossly slandered, we shall be comforted by remembering Him who did no sin, and in whose lips was found no guile. Our Lord Jesus is Head of the Guild of Sufferers: He did well, and suffered for it, but took it patiently. Our support under the cross, which we are appointed to bear, is only to be found in Him "who His own self bare our sins in His own body on the tree."

We ourselves now know by experience that there is no place for comfort like the cross. It is a tree stripped of all foliage, and apparently dead ; yet we sit under its shadow with great delight, and its fruit is sweet unto our taste. Truly, in this case, "like cures like." By the suffering of our Lord Jesus, our suffering is made light. The servant is comforted since Jesus took upon Himself the form of a servant ; the sufferer is cheered " because Christ also suffered for us ; " and the slandered one is strengthened because Jesus also was reviled.

> " Is it not strange, the darkest hour
>   That ever dawned on sinful earth
>   Should touch the heart with softer power
>   For comfort than an angel's mirth ?
>   That to the cross the mourner's eye should turn
>   Sooner than where the stars of Christmas burn ? "

Let us, as we hope to pass through the tribulations of this world, stand fast by the cross ; for if *that* be gone, the lone-star is quenched whose light cheers the down-trodden, shines on the injured, and brings light to the oppressed. If we lose the cross,—if we miss the substitutionary sacrifice of our Lord Jesus Christ, we have lost all.

The verse on which we would now devoutly meditate

speaks of three things : *the bearing of our sins,
the changing of our condition*, and *the healing of our
spiritual diseases*. Each of these deserves our most
careful notice.

I. The first is, THE BEARING OF OUR SINS by our
Lord : "Who His own self bare our sins in His own
body on the tree." These words in plainest terms
assert that our Lord Jesus did really bear the sins
of His people. How *literal* is the language ! Words
mean nothing if substitution is not stated here. I do
not know the meaning of the fifty-third of Isaiah if
this is not its meaning. Hear the prophet's words :
"The Lord hath laid on Him the iniquity of us all ; "
"for the transgression of my people was He stricken ; "
"He shall bear their iniquities :" "He was numbered
with the transgressors, and He bare the sin of many."

I cannot imagine that the Holy Spirit would have
used language so expressive if He had not intended
to teach us that our Saviour did really bear our sins,
and suffer in our stead. What else can be intended
by texts like these—"Christ was once offered to bear
the sins of many" (Heb. ix. 28) ; "He hath made
Him to be sin for us, who knew no sin ; that we might
be made the righteousness of God in Him " (2 Cor.
v. 21) ; "Christ hath redeemed us from the curse of
the law, being made a curse for us : for it is written,
Cursed is every one that hangeth on a tree " (Gal.
iii. 13) ; "Christ also hath loved us, and hath given
Himself for us an offering and a sacrifice to God for
a sweet-smelling savour " (Eph. v. 2) ; "Once in the
end of the world hath He appeared to put away sin
by the sacrifice of Himself" (Heb. ix. 26)? I say
modestly, but firmly, that these Scriptures either

teach the bearing of our sins by our Lord Jesus, or they teach nothing. In these days, among many errors and denials of truth, there has sprung up a teaching of "modern thought" which explains away the doctrine of substitution and vicarious sacrifice. One wise man has gone so far as to say that the transference of sin or righteousness is impossible, and another creature of the same school has stigmatized the idea as immoral.

It does not much matter what these modern haters of the cross may dare to say; but, assuredly, that which they deny, denounce, and deride, is the cardinal doctrine of our most holy faith, and is as clearly in Scripture as the sun is in the heavens. Beloved, as we suffer through the sin of Adam, so are we saved through the righteousness of Christ. Our fall was by another, and so is our rising again : we are under a system of representation and imputation, gainsay it who may. To us, the transference of our sin to Christ is a blessed fact clearly revealed in the Word of God, and graciously confirmed in the realizations of our faith. In that same chapter of Isaiah we read, "Surely He hath borne our griefs, and carried our sorrows," and we perceive that this was a matter of fact, for He was really, truly, and emphatically sorrowful ; and, therefore, when we read that "He bare our sins in His own body on the tree," we dare not fritter it away, but assuredly believe that in very deed He was our Sin-Bearer. Possible or impossible, we sing with full assurance—

"He bore on the tree the sentence for me."

Had the sorrow been figurative, the sin-bearing might

have been mythical; but the one fact is paralleled by the other. There is no figure in our text; it is a bare, literal fact: "Who His own self bare our sins in His own body on the tree." Oh, that men would give up cavilling! To question and debate at the cross, is an act near akin to the crime of the soldiers when they parted His garments among them, and cast lots for His vesture.

Note how *personal* are the terms here employed! How expressly the Holy Ghost speaketh! "Who His own self bare our sins in His own body." It was not by delegation, but "His own self"; and it was not in imagination, but "in His own body." Observe, also, the personality from our side of the question, He "bare *our* sins," that is to say, my sins and your sins. There is a sort of cadence of music here,—" His own self," "our sins." As surely as it was Christ's own self that suffered on the cross, so truly was it our own sins that Jesus bore in His own body on the tree. Our Lord has appeared in court for us, accepting our place at the bar: "He was numbered with the transgressors." Nay, more, He has appeared at the place of execution for us, and has borne the death-penalty upon the gibbet of doom in our stead. *In propriâ personâ*, our Redeemer has been arraigned, though innocent; has come under the curse, though for ever blessed; and has suffered to the death, though He had done nothing worthy of blame. "He was wounded for our transgressions, He was bruised for our iniquities: the chastisement of our peace was upon Him; and with His stripes we are healed."

This sin-bearing on our Lord's part was *continual*. The passage before us has been forced beyond its teaching, by being made to assert that our Lord Jesus bore our sins nowhere but on the cross: this the words do not say. "The tree" was the place where beyond all other places we see our Lord bearing the chastisement due to our sins; but before this, He had felt the weight of the enormous load. It is wrong to base a great doctrine upon the incidental form of one passage of Scripture, especially when that passage of Scripture bears another meaning.

The marginal reading, which is perfectly correct, is "Who His own self bare our sins in His own body *to* the tree." Our Lord carried the burden of our sins up to the tree, and there and then He made an end of it. He had carried that load long before, for John the Baptist said of Him, "Behold the Lamb of God, which taketh away" (the verb is in the present tense, "which taketh away") "the sin of the world" (John i. 29). Our Lord was then bearing the sin of the world as the Lamb of God. From the day when He began His divine ministry, I might say even before that, He bore our sins. He was the Lamb "slain from the foundation of the world;" so, when He went up to Calvary, bearing His cross, He was bearing our sins up to the tree. Yet, specially and peculiarly in His death-agony He stood in our stead, and upon His soul and body burst the tempest of justice which had gathered through our transgressions.

This sin-bearing is *final.* He bore our sins in His own body on the tree, but He bears them now no more. The sinner and the sinner's Surety are both free, for the law is vindicated, the honour of government is cleared, the substitutionary sacrifice is complete. He dieth no more, death hath no more dominion over Him ; for He has ended His work, and has cried, " It is finished." As for the sins which He bore in His own body on the tree, they cannot be found, for they have ceased to be, according to that ancient promise, " In those days, and in that time, saith the Lord, the iniquity of Israel shall be sought for, and there shall be none ; and the sins of Judah, and they shall not be found " (Jeremiah l. 20). The work of the Messiah was " to finish the transgression, and to make an end of sins, and to make reconciliation for iniquity, and to bring in everlasting righteousness " (Daniel ix. 24). Now, if sin is made an end of, there is an end of it ; and if transgression is "finished", there is no more to be said about it.

Let us look back with holy faith, and see Jesus bearing the stupendous load of our sins up to the tree, and on the tree ; and see how *effectual* was His sacrifice for discharging the whole mass of our moral liability both in reference to guiltiness in the sight of God, and the punishment which follows thereon. It is a law of nature that nothing can be in two places at the same time ; and if sin was borne away by our Lord, it cannot rest upon us. If by faith we have accepted the Substitute whom God Himself has accepted, then it cannot be that the penalty should be twice demanded, first of the Surety, and then of those for whom He stood. The Lord Jesus bore the sins of His people away, even as the scape-goat, in the type, carried the sin of Israel to a land uninhabited. Our sins are gone for ever. " As far as the east is from the west, so far hath He removed our transgressions from us." He hath cast all our iniquities into the depths of the sea ; he hath hurled them behind his back, where they shall no more be seen.

Beloved friends, we very calmly and coolly talk about this thing, but it is the greatest marvel in the universe; it is the miracle of earth, the mystery of heaven, the terror of hell. Could we fully realize the guilt of sin, the punishment due to it, and the literal substitution of Christ, it would work in us an intense enthusiasm of gratitude, love, and praise. I do not wonder that our Methodist friends shout, "Halle-lujah!" This is enough to make us all shout and sing, as long as we live, "Glory, glory to the Son of God!" What a wonder that the Prince of glory, in whom is no sin, who was indeed incapable of evil, should condescend to come into such contact with our sin as is implied in His being "made sin for us"! Our Lord Jesus did not handle sin with the golden tongs, but He bore it on His own shoulders. He did not lift it with golden staves, as the priests carried the ark; but He Himself bore the hideous load of our sin in His own body on the tree. This is the mystery of grace which angels desire to look into. I would for ever preach it in the plainest and most unmistak-able language.

II. In the second place, briefly notice THE CHANGE IN OUR CONDITION, which the text describes as coming out of the Lord's bearing of our sins: "That we, being dead to sins, should live unto righteousness." The change is a dying and a reviving, a burial and a resurrection: we are brought from life to death, and from death to life.

We are henceforth legally dead to the punishment of sin. If I were condemned to die for an offence, and some other died in my stead, then I died in him who died for me. The law could not a second time lay its charge against me, and bring me again before the judge, and condemn me, and lead me out to die. Where would be the justice of such a procedure? I am dead already: how can I die again? I have borne the wrath of God in the person of my glorious and ever-blessed Substitute; how then can I bear it again? Where was the use of a Substitute if I am to bear it also? Should Satan come before God to lay an accusation against me, the answer is, " This man is dead. He has borne the penalty, and is 'dead to sins,' for the sentence against him has been executed upon Another." What a wonderful deliverance for us! Bless the Lord, O my soul!

But Peter also means to remind us that, by and through the influence of Christ's death upon our hearts, *the Holy Ghost has made us now to be actually "dead to sins"*: that is to say, we no longer love them, and they have ceased to hold dominion over us. Sin is no longer at home in our hearts; if it enters there, it is as an intruder. We are no more its willing servants. Sin calls to us by temptation, but we give it no answer, for we are dead to its voice. Sin promises us a high reward, but we do not consent, for we are dead to its allurements. We sin, but our will is not to sin. It would be heaven to us to be perfectly holy. Our heart and life go after perfection, but sin is abhorred of our soul. "Now, if I do that which I would not, it is no more I that do it, but sin that dwelleth in me." Our truest and most real self loathes sin; and though we fall into it, it is a fall,— we are out of our element, and escape from the evil with all speed. The new-born life within us has no dealings with sin ; it is dead to sin.

The Greek word here used cannot be fully rendered into English ; it signifies " being unborn to sins." We were born in sin, but by the death of Christ, and the work of the Holy Spirit upon us, that birth is undone, " we are unborn to sins." That which was wrought in us by sin, even at our birth, is through the death of Jesus counteracted by the new life which His Spirit imparts. "We are unborn to sins." I like the phrase, unusual as it sounds. Does it seem possible that birth should be reversed : the born unborn ? Yet so it is. The true *ego*, the reallest " I," is now unborn to sins, for we are " born, not of blood, nor of the will of the flesh, nor of the will of man, but of God." We are unborn to sins, and born unto God.

But our Lord's sin-bearing has also *brought us into life*. Dead to evil according to law, we also live in newness of life in the kingdom of grace. Our Lord's object is "that we should live unto righteousness." Not only are our lives to be righteous, which I trust they are, but we are quickened and made sensitive and vigorous unto righteousness : through our Lord's death we are made quick of eye, and quick of thought, and quick of lip, and quick of heart unto righteousness. Certainly, if the doctrine of His atoning sacrifice does not vivify us, nothing will. When we sin, it is the sorrowful result of our former death ; but when we work righteousness, we throw our whole soul into it, "We live unto righteousness." Because our Divine Lord has died, we feel that we must lay ourselves out for His praise. The tree which brought death to our Saviour is a tree of life to us. Sit under this true *arbor vitæ*, and you will shake off the weakness and disease which came in by that tree of knowledge of good and evil. Livingstone in Africa used certain medicines which are known as *Livingstone's Rousers;* but what rousers are those glorious truths which are extracted from the bitter wood of the cross! O my brethren, let us show in our lives what wonders our Lord Jesus has done for us by His agony and bloody sweat, by His cross and passion!

III. The apostle then speaks of THE HEALING OF OUR DISEASES by Christ's death: "By whose stripes ye were healed. For ye were as sheep going astray; but are now returned unto the Shepherd and Bishop of your souls."

We were healed, and we remain so. It is not a thing to be done in the future; it has been wrought. Peter describes our disease in the words which compose verse twenty-five. What was it, then?

First, it was *brutishness.* "Ye were as sheep." Sin has made us so that we are only fit to be compared to beasts, and to those of the least intelligence. Sometimes the Scripture compares the unregenerate man to an ass. Man is said to be "born like a wild ass's colt." Amos likens Israel to the "kine of Bashan", and he saith to them, "Ye shall go out at the breaches, every cow at that which is before her." David compared himself to behemoth: "So foolish was I, and ignorant: I was as a beast before Thee." We are nothing better than beasts until Christ comes to us. But we are not beasts after that: a living, heavenly, spiritual nature is created within us when we come into contact with our Redeemer. We still carry about with us the old brutish nature, but by the grace of God it is put in subjection, and kept there ; and our fellowship now is with the Father, and with His Son Jesus Christ. We "were as sheep," but we are now men redeemed unto God.

We are cured also of the *proneness to wander* which is so remarkable in sheep. "Ye were as sheep going astray," always going astray, loving to go astray, delighting in it, never so happy as when they are wandering away from the fold. We wander still, but not as sheep wander : we now seek the right way, and desire to follow the Lamb whithersoever He goeth. If we wander, it is through ignorance or temptation. We can truly say, "My soul followeth hard after Thee." Our Lord's cross has nailed us fast as to hands and feet : we cannot now run greedily after iniquity ; rather do we say, "Return unto thy rest, O my soul ; for the Lord hath dealt bountifully with thee ! "

> " My wanderings, Lord, are at an end,
>   I'm now return'd to Thee :
>   Be Thou my Father and my Friend,
>   Be all in all to me."

Another disease of ours was *inability to return :* "Ye were as sheep going astray ; but are now returned." Dogs and even swine are more likely to return home than wandering sheep. But now, beloved, though we wandered, we have returned, and do still return to our Shepherd. Like Noah's dove, we have found no rest for the sole of our foot anywhere out of the ark, and therefore we return unto Him, and He graciously pulls us in unto Him. If we wander at any time, we bless God that there is a sacred something within us which will not let us rest, and there is a far more powerful something above us which draws us back. We are like the needle in the compass : touch that needle with your finger, and compel it to point to the east, or to the south, and it may do so for the moment ; but take away the pressure, and in an instant it returns to the pole. So we must go back to Jesus ; we must return to the Bishop of our souls. Our soul cries, " Whom have I in heaven but Thee ? and there is none upon earth that I desire beside Thee." Thus, by the virtue of our Lord's death, an immortal love is created in us, which leads us to seek His face, and renew our fellowship with Him.

Our Lord's death has also cured us of our *readiness to follow other leaders.* If one sheep goes through a gap in the hedge, the whole flock will follow. We have been accustomed to follow ringleaders in sin, or in error : we have been too ready to follow custom, and to do that which is judged proper, respectable, and usual : but now we are resolved to follow none but Jesus, according to His word, " My sheep hear My voice, and I know them, and they follow Me. A stranger will they not follow, but will flee from him : for they know not the voice of strangers." For my own part, I am resolved to follow no human leader. Faith in Jesus creates a sacred independence of mind. We have learned so entire a dependence upon our crucified Lord that we have none to spare for men.

Finally, beloved friends, when we were wandering we were like sheep *exposed to wolves*, but we are delivered from this by being near the Shepherd. We were in danger of death, in danger from the devil, in danger from a thousand temptations, which, like ravenous beasts, prowled around us. Having ended our wandering, we are now in a place of safety. When the lion roars, we are driven the closer to the Shepherd, and rejoice that His crook protects us. He says, " My sheep hear My voice, and I know them, and they follow Me : and I give unto them eternal life ; and they shall never perish, neither shall any man pluck them out of My hand."

What a wonderful work of grace has been wrought in us ! We owe all this, not to the teaching of Christ, though that has helped us greatly ; not to the example of Christ, though that is charming us into a diligent copying of it ; but we owe it all to His stripes : " By whose stripes ye were healed." Brethren, we preach Christ crucified, because we have been saved by Christ crucified. His death is the death of our sins. We can never give up the doctrine of Christ's substitutionary sacrifice, for it is the power by which we hope to be made holy. Not only are we washed from guilt in His blood, but by that blood we overcome sin. Never, so long as breath or pulse remains, can we conceal the blessed truth that He " His own self bare our sins in His own body on the tree, that we, being dead to sins, should live unto righteousness." The Lord give us to know much more of this than I can speak, for Jesus Christ's sake ! Amen.

" Fear not : for I have redeemed thee."—*Isaiah* xliii. 1.

7

Redeemed Souls Freed from Fear

I WAS lamenting this morning my unfitness for my work, and especially for the warfare to which I am called. A sense of heaviness came over me, but relief came very speedily, for which I thank the Lord. Indeed, I was greatly burdened, but the Lord succoured me. The first verse read at the Sabbath morning service exactly met my case. It is in Isaiah xliii. 1: "But now thus saith the Lord that created thee, O Jacob, and He that formed thee, O Israel, Fear not." I said to myself, "I am what God created me, and I am what He formed me, and therefore I must, after all, be the right man for the place wherein He has put me." We may not blame our Creator, nor suspect that He has missed His mark in forming an instrument for His work. Thus new comfort comes to us. Not only do the operations of grace in the spiritual world yield us consolation, but we are even comforted by what the Lord has done in creation. We are told to cease from our fears ; and we do so, since we perceive that it is the Lord that made us, and not we ourselves, and He will justify His own creating skill by accomplishing through us the purposes of His love. Pray, I beseech you, for me, the weakest of my Lord's servants, that I may be equal to the overwhelming task imposed upon me.

The next sentence of the chapter is usually most

comforting to my soul, although on this one occasion
the first sentence was a specially reviving cordial to
me. The verse goes on to say,—

> " *Fear not : for I have redeemed thee.*"

Let us think for a few minutes of the wonderful
depth of consolation which lies in this fact. We have
been redeemed by the Lord Himself, and this is a
grand reason why we should never again be subject to
fear. Oh, that the logic of this fact could be turned
into practice, so that we henceforth rejoiced, or at
least felt the peace of God !

These words may be spoken, first of all, of those
frequent occasions in which the Lord has redeemed
His people out of *trouble.* Many a time and oft might
our Lord say to each one of us, " I have redeemed
thee." Out of six, yea, six thousand trials He has
brought us forth by the right hand of His power. He
has released us from our afflictions, and brought us
forth into a wealthy place. In the remembrance of
all these redemptions the Lord seems to say to us,
" What I have done before, I will do again. I have
redeemed thee, and I will still redeem thee. I have
brought thee from under the hand of the oppressor ;
I have delivered thee from the tongue of the slanderer ;
I have borne thee up under the load of poverty, and
sustained thee under the pains of sickness ; and I am
able still to do the same : wherefore, then, dost thou
fear ? Why shouldst thou be afraid, since already I
have again and again redeemed thee ? Take heart,
and be confident ; for even to old age and to death
itself I will continue to be thy strong Redeemer."

I suppose there would be a reference here to the

great redemption out of Egypt. This word is addressed to the people of God under captivity in Babylon, and we know that the Lord referred to the Egyptian redemption ; for He says in the third verse, " I gave Egypt for thy ransom." Egypt was a great country, and a rich country, for we read of " all the treasures of Egypt", but God gave them for His chosen : He would give all the nations of the earth for His Israel. This was a wonderful stay to the people of God : they constantly referred to Egypt and the Red Sea, and made their national song out of it. In all Israel's times of disaster, and calamity, and trial, they joyfully remembered that the Lord had redeemed them when they were a company of slaves, helpless and hopeless, under a tyrant who cast their firstborn children into the Nile, a tyrant whose power was so tremendous that all the armies of the world could not have wrought their deliverance from his iron hand. The very nod of Pharaoh seemed to the inhabitants of Egypt to be omnipotent ; he was a builder of pyramids, a master of all the sciences of peace and the arts of war. What could the Israelites have done against him ? Jehovah came to their relief in their dire extremity. His plagues followed each other in quick succession. The dread volleys of the Lord's artillery confounded His foes. At last He smote all the firstborn of Egypt, the chief of all their strength. Then was Egypt glad that Israel departed, and the Lord brought forth His people with silver and gold. All the chivalry of Egypt was overthrown and destroyed at the Red Sea, and the timbrels of the daughters of Israel sounded joyously upon its shores. This redemption out of Egypt is so remarkable that it is remembered even in heaven. The Old Testament song is woven into that of the New Covenant; for there they "sing the song of Moses the servant of God, and the song of the Lamb." The first redemption was so wonderful a type and prophecy of the other that it is no alloy to the golden hymn of eternal glory, but readily melts into the same celestial chant. Other types may cease to be remembered, but this was so much a fact as well as a type that it shall be had in memory for ever and ever. Every Israelite ought to have had confidence in God after what He had done for the people in redeeming them out of Egypt. To every one of the seed of Jacob it was a grand argument to enforce the precept, " Fear not."

But I take it that the chief reference of these words is to that redemption which has been wrought out for us by Him who loved us, and washed us from our sins in His own blood. Let us think of it for a minute or two before we break the bread and drink of the cup of communion.

The remembrance of this transcendent redemption ought to comfort us in all times of *perplexity*. When we cannot see our way, or cannot make out what to do, we need not be at all troubled concerning it ; for the Lord Jehovah can see a way out of every intricacy. There never was a problem so hard to solve as that which is answered in redemption. Herein was the tremendous difficulty—How can God be just, and yet be the Saviour of sinners? How can He fulfil His threatenings; and yet forgive sin? If that problem had been left to angels and men, they could never have worked it out throughout eternity ; but God has solved it through freely delivering up His own Son. In the glorious sacrifice of Jesus we see the justice of God magnified ; for He laid sin on the blessed Lord, who had become one with His chosen. Jesus identified Himself with His people, and therefore their sin was laid upon Him, and the sword of the Lord awoke against Him. He was not taken arbitrarily to be a victim, but He was a voluntary Sufferer. His relationship amounted to covenant oneness with His people, and " it behoved Christ to suffer." Herein is a wisdom which must be more than equal to all minor perplexities. Hear this, then, O poor soul in suspense ! The Lord says, " I have redeemed thee. I have already brought thee out of the labyrinth in which thou wast lost by sin, and therefore I will take thee out of the meshes of the net of temptation, and lead thee through the maze of trial ; I will bring the blind by a way that they know not, and lead them in paths which they have not known. I will bring again from Bashan, I will bring up My people from the depths of the sea." Let us commit our way unto the Lord. Mine is a peculiarly difficult one, but I know that my Redeemer liveth, and He will lead me by a right way. He will be our Guide even unto death ; and after death He will guide us through those tracks unknown of the mysterious region, and cause us to rest with Him for ever.

So also, if at any time we are in great *poverty*, or in great straitness of means for the Lord's work, and we are, therefore, afraid that we shall never get our needs supplied, let us cast off such fears as we listen to the music of these words : " Fear not: for I have redeemed thee." God Himself looked down from heaven, and saw that there was no man who could give to Him a ransom for his brother, and each man on his own part was hopelessly bankrupt; and then, despite our spiritual beggary, He found the means of our redemption. What then? Let us hear the use which the Holy Spirit makes of this fact: " He that spared not His own Son, but delivered Him up for us all, how shall He not with Him also freely give us all things?" We cannot have a want which the Lord will not supply. Since God has given us Jesus, He will give us, not some things, but "all things." Indeed, all things are ours in Christ Jesus. No necessity of this life can for a single moment be compared to that dread necessity which the Lord has already supplied. The infinite gift of God's own Son is a far greater one than all that can be included in the term "all things": wherefore, it is a grand argument to the poor and needy, " Fear not: for I have redeemed thee." Perplexity and poverty are thus effectually met.

We are at times troubled by a sense of our personal *insignificance*. It seems too much to hope that God's infinite mind should enter into our mean affairs. Though David said, " I am poor and needy, yet the Lord thinketh upon me," we are not always quite prepared to say the same. We make our sorrows great under the vain idea that they are too small for the Lord to notice. I believe that our greatest miseries spring from those little worries which we hesitate to bring to our heavenly Father. Our gracious God puts an end to all such thoughts as these by saying, " Fear not: for I have redeemed thee." You are not of such small account as you suppose. The Lord would never be wasteful of His sacred expenditure.

He bought you with a price, and therefore He sets great store by you. Listen to what the Lord says : " Since thou wast precious in My sight, thou hast been honourable, and I have loved thee : therefore will I give men for thee, and people for thy life." It is amazing that the Lord should think so much of us as to give Jesus for us. "What is man that Thou art mindful of him ? " Yet God's mind is filled with thoughts of love towards man. Know ye not that His only-begotten Son entered this world, and became a man ? The man Christ Jesus has a name at which every knee shall bow, and He is so dear to the Father that, for His sake, His chosen ones are accepted, and are made to enjoy the freest access to Him. We sing truly,—

> " So near, so very near to God,
>   Nearer we cannot be,
> For in the person of His Son
>   We are as near as He."

And now the very hairs of our head are all numbered, and the least burden we may roll upon the Lord. Those cares which we ought not to have may well cease, for " He careth for us." He that redeemed us never forgets us : His wounds have graven us upon the palms of His hands, and written our names deep in His side. Jesus stoops to our level, for He stooped to bear the cross to redeem us. Do not, therefore, be again afraid because of your insignificance. "Why sayest thou, O Jacob, and speakest, O Israel, My way is hid from the Lord, and my judgment is passed over from my God ? Hast thou not known ? Hast thou not heard, that the everlasting God, the Lord, the Creator of the ends of the earth, fainteth not, neither is weary? There is no searching of His understanding. He giveth power to the faint; and to them that have no might He increaseth strength." The Lord's memory is toward the little in Israel. He carrieth the lambs in His bosom.

We are liable to fret a little when we think of our *changeableness.* If you are at all like me, you are very far from being always alike; I am sometimes lifted up to the very heavens, and then I go down to the deeps; I am at one time bright with joy and confidence, and at another time dark as midnight with doubts and fears. Even Elijah, who was so brave, had his fainting fits. We are to be blamed for this, and yet the fact remains: our experience is as an April day, when shower and sunshine take their turns. Amid our mournful changes we rejoice to hear the Lord's own voice, saying, "Fear not: for I have redeemed thee." Everything is not changeful wave; there is rock somewhere. Redemption is a fact accomplished.

"The Cross, it standeth fast. Hallelujah!"

The price is paid, the ransom accepted. This is done, and can never be undone. Jesus says, "I have redeemed thee." Change of feeling within does not alter the fact that the believer has been bought with a price, and made the Lord's own by the precious blood of Jesus. The Lord God has already done so much for us that our salvation is sure in Christ Jesus. Will He begin to build, and fail to finish? Will He lay the foundation in the everlasting covenant? Will He dedicate the walls with the infinite sacrifice of the Lamb of God? Will He give up the choicest treasure He ever had, the chosen of God and precious, to be the corner-stone, and then not finish the work He has begun ? It is impossible. If He has redeemed us, He has, in that act, given us the pledge of all things.

See how the gifts of God are bound to this redemption. "I have redeemed thee. I have called thee." "For whom He did foreknow, He also did predestinate to be conformed to the image of His Son, that He might be the firstborn among many brethren. Moreover whom He did predestinate, them He also called : and whom He called, them He also justified : and whom He justified, them He also glorified." Here is a chain in which each link is joined to all the rest, so that it cannot be separated. If God had only gone so far as to make a promise, He would not have drawn back from it ; if God had gone as far as to swear an oath by Himself, He would not have failed to keep it ; but when He went beyond promise and oath, and in very deed the sacrifice was slain, and the covenant was ratified : why, then it would be blasphemous to imagine that He would afterwards disannul it, and turn from His solemn pledge. There is no going back on the part of God, and consequently His redemption will redeem, and in redeeming it will secure us all things. "Who shall separate us from the love of Christ ? " With the blood-mark upon us we may well cease to fear. How can we perish ? How can we be deserted in the hour of need ? We have been bought with too great a price for our Redeemer to let us slip. Therefore, let us march on with confidence, hearing our Redeemer say to us, " When thou passest through the waters, I will be with thee ; and through the rivers, they shall not overflow thee : when thou walkest through the fire, thou shalt not be burned; neither shall the flame kindle upon thee." Concerning His redeemed, the Lord will say to the enemy, "Touch not Mine anointed, and do My prophets no harm." The stars in their courses fight for the ransomed of the Lord. If their eyes were opened, they would see the mountain full of horses of fire and chariots of fire round about them. Oh, how my weary heart prizes redeeming love! If it were not for this, I would lay me down, and die. Friends forsake me, foes surround me, I am filled with contempt, and tortured with the subtlety which I cannot baffle; but as the Lord of all brought again from the dead our Lord Jesus, that great Shepherd of the sheep, by the blood of the everlasting covenant, so by the blood of His covenant doth He loose His prisoners, and sustain the hearts of those who tremble at His Word. "O my soul, thou hast trodden down strength," for the Lord hath said unto thee, "Fear not: for I have redeemed thee."

" I will not leave you comfortless : I will come to you."—*John* xiv. 18.

8

The Believer Not an Orphan

YOU will notice that the margin reads, "I will not leave you orphans : I will come to you." In the absence of our Lord Jesus Christ, the disciples were like children deprived of their parents. During the three years in which He had been with them, He had solved all their difficulties, borne all their burdens, and supplied all their needs. Whenever a case was too hard or too heavy for them, they took it to Him. When their enemies well nigh overcame them, Jesus came to the rescue, and turned the tide of battle. They were all happy and safe enough whilst the Master was with them ; He walked in their midst like a father amid a large family of children, making all the household glad. But now He was about to be taken from them by an ignominious death, and they might well feel that they would be like little children deprived of their natural and beloved protector. Our Saviour knew the fear that was in their hearts, and before they could express it, He removed it by saying, "You shall not be left alone in this wild and desert world ; though I be absent in the flesh, yet I will be present with you in a more efficacious manner ; I will come to you spiritually, and you shall derive from My spiritual presence even more good than you could have had from My bodily presence, had I still continued in your midst."

Observe, first, here is *an evil averted:* " I will not leave you orphans ; " and, in the second place, here is *a consolation provided:* " I will come to you."

I.   First, here is, AN EVIL AVERTED.

Without their Lord, believers would, apart from the Holy Spirit, be like other orphans, unhappy and desolate.   Give them what you might, their loss could not have been recompensed.   No number of lamps can make up for the sun's absence ; blaze as they may, it is still night.   No circle of friends can supply to a bereaved woman the loss of her husband ; without him, she is still a widow.   Even thus, without Jesus, it is inevitable that the saints should be as orphans ; but Jesus has promised in the text that we shall not be so ; the one only thing that can remove the trial He declares shall be ours, " I will come to you."

Now remember, that *an orphan is one whose parent is dead.*   This in itself is a great sorrow, if there were no other.   The dear father, so well beloved, was suddenly smitten down with sickness ; they watched him with anxiety ; they nursed him with sedulous care ; but he expired.   The loving eye is closed in darkness for them.   That active hand will no longer toil for the family.   That heart and brain will no longer feel and think for them.   Beneath the green grass the father sleeps, and every time the child surveys that hallowed hillock his heart swells with grief.   Beloved, we are not orphans in that sense, for our Lord Jesus is not dead.   It is true He died, for one of the soldiers with a spear pierced His side, and forthwith came thereout blood and water, a sure evidence that the pericardium had been pierced, and that the fountain of life had been broken up.   He died, 'tis certain, but He is not

114

dead now. Go not to the grave to seek Him. Angel voices say, "He is not here, for He is risen." He could not be holden by the bands of death. We do not worship a dead Christ, nor do we even think of Him now as a corpse. That picture on the wall, which the Romanists paint and worship, represents Christ as dead; but oh! it is so good to think of Christ as living, remaining in an existence real and true, none the less living because He died, but all the more truly full of life because He has passed through the portals of the grave, and is now reigning for ever. See then, dear friends, the bitter root of the orphan's sorrow is gone from us, for our Jesus is not dead now. No mausoleum enshrines His ashes, no pyramid entombs His body, no monument records the place of His permanent sepulchre.

> "He lives, the great Redeemer lives,
>   What joy the blest assurance gives!"

We are not orphans, for "the Lord is risen indeed."

The orphan has a sharp sorrow springing out of the death of his parent, namely, that *he is left alone.* He cannot now make appeals to the wisdom of the parent who could direct him. He cannot run, as once he did, when he was weary, to climb the paternal knee. He cannot lean his aching head upon the parental bosom. "Father," he may say, but no voice gives an answer. "Mother," he may cry, but that fond title, which would awaken the mother if she slept, cannot arouse her from the bed of death. The child is alone, alone as to those two hearts which were its best companions. The parent and lover are gone. The little ones know what it is to be deserted and forsaken. But we are not so; we are not orphans. It is true Jesus is not here in body, but His spiritual presence is quite as blessed as His bodily presence would have been. Nay, it is better, for supposing Jesus Christ to be here in person, you could not all come and touch the hem of His garment,—not all at once, at any rate. There might be thousands waiting all the world over to speak with Him ; but how could they all reach Him, if He were merely here in body? You might all be wanting to tell Him something, but in the body He could only receive some one or two of you at a time.

But in spirit there is no need for you to stir from the pew, no need to say a word ; Jesus hears your thoughts talk, and attends to all your needs at the same moment. No need to press to get at Him because the throng is great, for He is as near to me as He is to you, and as near to you as to saints in America, or the islands of the Southern Sea. He is everywhere present, and all His beloved may talk with Him. You can tell Him at this moment the sorrows which you dare not open up to anyone else. You will feel that, in declaring them to Him, you have not breathed them to the air, but that a real Person has heard you, One as real as though you could grip His hand, and could see the loving flash of His eye and mark the sympathetic change of His countenance.

Is it not so with you, ye children of a living Saviour ? You know it is ; you have a Friend that sticketh closer than a brother. You have a near and dear One, who, in the dead of the night is in the chamber, and in the heat and burden of the day is in the field of labour. You are not orphans, the "Wonderful, Counsellor, the mighty God, the Everlasting Father, the Prince of Peace," is with you ; your Lord is here ; and, as one whom his mother comforteth, so Jesus comforts you.

The orphan, too, has *lost the kind hand which took care always that food and raiment should be provided, that the table should be well stored, and that the house should be kept in comfort.* Poor feeble one, who will provide for his wants? His father is dead, his mother is gone : who will take care of the little wanderer now? But it is not so with us. Jesus has not left us orphans; His care for His people is no less now than it was when He sat at the table with Mary, and Martha, and Lazarus, whom "Jesus loved." Instead of the provisions being less, they are even greater, for since the Holy Spirit has been given to us, we have richer fare and are more indulged with spiritual comforts than believers were before the bodily presence of the Master had departed. Do your souls hunger to-night? Jesus gives you the bread of heaven. Do you thirst to-night? The waters from the rock cease not to flow.

" Come, make your wants, your burdens known."

You have but to make known your needs to have them all supplied, Christ waits to be gracious in the midst of this assembly. He is here with His golden hand, opening that hand to supply the wants of every living soul. "Oh !" saith one, " I am poor and needy." Go on with the quotation. "Yet the Lord thinketh upon me." "Ah !" saith another, " I have besought the Lord thrice to take away a thorn in the flesh from me." Remember what he said to Paul, " My grace is sufficient for thee." You are not left without the strength you want. The Lord is your

Shepherd still. He will provide for you till He leads you through death's dark valley, and brings you to the shining pastures upon the hill-tops of glory. You are not destitute, you need not beg an asylum from an ungodly world by bowing to its demands, or trusting its vain promises, for Jesus will never leave you nor forsake you.

The orphan, too, is *left without the instruction which is most suitable for a child*. We may say what we will, but there is none so fit to form a child's character as the parent. It is a very sad loss for a child to have lost either father or mother in its early days ; for the most skilful preceptor, though he may do much, by the blessing of God very much, is but a stop-gap, and but half makes up for the original ordinance of Providence, that the parent's love should fashion the child's mind. But, dear friends, we are not orphans ; we who believe in Jesus are not left without an education. Jesus is not here Himself, it is true. I dare say some of you wish you could come on Lord's-days, and listen to Him ! Would it not be sweet to look up to this pulpit, and see the Crucified One, and to hear Him preach ? Ah ! so you think, but the apostle says, " Though we have known Christ after the flesh, yet now henceforth know we Him no more."

It is most for your profit that you should receive the Spirit of truth, not through the golden vessel of Christ in His actual presence here, but through the poor earthen vessels of humble servants of God like ourselves. At any rate, whether *we* speak, or an angel from heaven, the speaker matters not ; it is the Spirit of God alone that is the power of the Word, and makes that Word to become vital and quickening to you. Now, you have the Spirit of God. The Holy Spirit is so given, that there is not a truth which you may not understand. You may be led into the deepest mysteries by His teaching. You may be made to know and to comprehend those knotty points in the Word of God which have hitherto puzzled you. You have but humbly to look up to Jesus, and His Spirit will still teach you. I tell you, though you are poor and ignorant, and perhaps can scarcely read a word in the Bible ; for all that, you may be better instructed in the things of God than doctors of divinity, if you go to the Holy Spirit, and are taught of Him. Those who go only to books and to the letter, and are taught of men, may be fools in the sight of God ; but those who go to Jesus, and sit at His feet, and ask to be taught of His Spirit, shall be wise unto salvation. Blessed be God, there are not a few amongst us of this sort. We are not left orphans ; we have an Instructor with us still.

There is one point in which the orphan is often sorrowfully reminded of his orphanhood, namely, *in lacking a defender.* It is so natural in little children, when some big boy molests them, to say, " I'll tell my father !" How often did we use to say so, and how often have we heard from the little ones since, " I'll tell mother !" Sometimes, the not being able to do this is a much severer loss than we can guess. Unkind and cruel men have snatched away from orphans the little which a father's love had left behind ; and in the court of law there has been no defender to protect the orphan's goods. Had the father been there, the child would have had its rights, scarcely would any have dared to infringe them ; but, in the absence of the father, the orphan is eaten up like bread, and the wicked of the earth devour his estate. In this sense, the saints are not orphans. The devil would rob us of our heritage if he could, but there is an Advocate with the Father who pleads for us. Satan would snatch from us every promise, and tear from us all the comforts of the covenant; but we are not orphans, and when he brings a suit-at-law against us, and thinks that we are the only defendants in the case, he is mistaken, for we have an Advocate on high. Christ comes in and pleads, as the sinners' Friend, for us; and when *He* pleads at the bar of justice, there is no fear but that His plea will be of effect, and our inheritance shall be safe. He has not left us orphans.

Now I want, without saying many words, to get you who love the Master to feel what a very precious thought this is, that you are not alone in this world; that, if you have no earthly friends, if you have none to whom you can take your cares, if you are quite lonely so far as outward friends are concerned, yet Jesus is with you, is really with you, practically with you, able to help you, and ready to do so, and that you have a good and kind Protector close at hand at this present moment, for Christ has said it: " I will not leave you orphans."

II. Secondly, there is, A CONSOLATION PROVIDED. The remedy by which the evil is averted is this, our Lord Jesus said, " *I will come to you.*"

What does this mean? Does it not mean, from the connection, this—" *I will come to you by My Spirit* "? Beloved, we must not confuse the Persons of the Godhead. The Holy Spirit is not the Son of God; Jesus, the Son of God, is not the Holy Spirit.

They are two distinct Persons of the one Godhead. But yet there is such a wonderful unity, and the blessed Spirit acts so marvellously as the Vicar of Christ, that it is quite correct to say that, when the Spirit comes, Jesus comes, too, and "I will come to you," means— "I, by My Spirit, who shall take My place, and represent Me, I will come to be with you." See then, Christian, you have the Holy Spirit in you and with you to be the Representative of Christ. Christ is with you now, not in person, but by His Representative, —an efficient, almighty, divine, everlasting Representative, who stands for Christ, and is as Christ to you in His presence in your souls. Because you thus have Christ by His Spirit, you cannot be orphans, for the Spirit of God is always with you. It is a delightful truth that the Spirit of God always dwells in believers ; —not sometimes, but always. He is not always active in believers, and He may be grieved until His sensible presence is altogether withdrawn, but His secret presence is always there. At no single moment is the Spirit of God wholly gone from a believer. The believer would die spiritually if this could happen, but that cannot be, for Jesus has said, "Because I live, ye shall live also." Even when the believer sins, the Holy Spirit does not utterly depart from him, but is still in him to make him smart for the sin into which he has fallen. The believer's prayers prove that the Holy Spirit is still within him. "Take not Thy Holy Spirit from me," was the prayer of a saint who had fallen very foully, but in whom the Spirit of God still kept His residence, notwithstanding all the foulness of his guilt and sin.

But, beloved, in addition to this, Jesus Christ by

His Spirit *makes visits to His people of a peculiar kind.* The Holy Ghost becomes wonderfully active and potent at certain times of refreshing. We are then especially and joyfully sensible of His divine power. His influence streams through every chamber of our nature, and floods our dark soul with His glorious rays, as the sun shining in its strength. Oh, how delightful this is! Sometimes we have felt this at the Lord's table. My soul pants to sit with you at that table, because I do remember many a happy time when the emblems of bread and wine have assisted my faith, and kindled the passions of my soul into a heavenly flame. I am equally sure that, at the prayer-meeting, under the preaching of the Word, in private meditation, and in searching the Scriptures, we can say that Jesus Christ has come to us. What! have you no hill Mizar to remember?—

> "No Tabor-visits to recount,
> When with Him in the Holy Mount"?

Oh, yes! some of these blessed seasons have left their impress upon our memories, so that, amongst our dying thoughts, will mingle the remembrance of those blessed seasons when Jesus Christ manifested Himself unto us as He doth not unto the world. Oh, to be wrapped in that crimson vest, closely pressed to His open side! Oh, to put our finger into the print of nails, and thrust our hand into His side! We know what this means by past experience.

> "Dear Shepherd of Thy chosen few,
> Thy former mercies here renew."

Permit us once again to feel the truth of the promise, "I will not leave you orphans; I will come to you,"

And now, gathering up the few thoughts I have uttered, let me remind you, dear friends, that *every word of the text is instructive :* " I will not leave you orphans : I will come to you." Observe the " I " there twice over. " *I* will not leave you orphans ; father and mother may, but *I* will not ; friends once beloved may turn stony-hearted, but *I* will not ; Judas may play the traitor, and Ahithophel may betray his David, but *I* will not leave you comfortless. You have had many disappointments, great heart-breaking sorrows, but *I* have never caused you any ; *I*—the faithful and the true Witness, the immutable, the unchangeable Jesus, the same yesterday, to-day, and for ever, *I* will not leave you comfortless ; *I* will come unto you." Catch at that word, " I," and let your souls say, " Lord, I am not worthy that Thou shouldest come under my roof ; if Thou hadst said, ' I will send an angel to thee,' it would have been a great mercy, but what sayest Thou, ' I will come unto thee ' ? If Thou hadst bidden some of my brethren come and speak a word of comfort to me, I had been thankful, but Thou hast put it thus in the first person, ' *I* will come unto you.' O my Lord, what shall I say, what shall I do, but feel a hungering and a thirsting after Thee, which nothing shall satisfy till Thou shalt fulfil Thine own Word, ' *I* will not leave you comfortless ; *I* will come to you ' " ?

And then notice the persons to whom it is addressed, " I will not leave *you* comfortless, you, Peter, who will deny Me ; *you*, Thomas, who will doubt Me ; I will not leave *you* comfortless." O you who are so little in Israel that you sometimes think it is a pity that your name is in the church-book at all, because you feel yourselves to be so worthless, so unworthy, He will not leave *you* comfortless, not even *you!* "O Lord," thou sayest, "if Thou wouldst look after the rest of Thy sheep, I would bless Thee for Thy tenderness to them, but *I*—I deserve to be left; if I were forsaken of Thee, I could not blame Thee, for I have played the harlot against Thy love, but yet Thou sayest, 'I will not leave *you.*'" Heir of heaven, do not lose your part in this promise. I pray you say, "Lord, come unto me, and though Thou refresh all my brethren, yet, Lord, refresh me with some of the droppings of Thy love; O Lord, fill the cup *for me; my* thirsty spirit pants for it.

> "'I thirst, I faint, I die to prove
> The greatness of redeeming love,
> The love of Christ to me.'

Now, Lord, fulfil Thy word to Thine unworthy handmaid, as I stand like Hannah in Thy presence. Come unto me, Thy servant, unworthy to lift so much as his eyes towards heaven, and only daring to say, 'God be merciful to me a sinner.' Fulfil Thy promise even to me, 'I will not leave you comfortless; I will come to you.'"

Take whichever of the words you will, and they each one sparkle and flash after this sort. Observe, too, *the richness and sufficiency of the text:* "I will not leave you comfortless: I will come to you." He does not promise, "I will send you sanctifying grace, or sustaining mercy, or precious mercy," but He says, what is the only thing that will prevent your being orphans, "I will come to you." Ah! Lord, Thy grace is sweet, but Thou art better. The vine is good, but the clusters are better. It is well enough to have a gift from Thy hand, but oh! to touch the hand itself. It is well enough to hear the words of Thy lips, but oh! to kiss those lips as the spouse did in the Song, this is better still. You know, if there be an orphan child, you cannot prevent its continuing an orphan. You may feel great kindness towards it, supply its wants, and do all you possibly can towards it, but it is an orphan still. It must get its father and its mother back, or else it will still be an orphan. So, our blessed Lord, knowing this, does not say, " I will do this and that for you," but, " I will come to you."

Do you not see, dear friends, here is not only all you can want, but all you think you can want, wrapped up in a sentence, " I will come to you " ?   " It pleased the Father that in Him should all fulness dwell ; " so that, when Christ comes, in Him " all fulness" comes.   " In Him dwelleth all the fulness of the Godhead bodily," so that, when Jesus comes, the very Godhead comes to the believer.

> " All my capacious powers can wish
> In Thee doth richly meet ; "

and if Thou shalt come to me, it is better than all the gifts of Thy covenant. If I get Thee, I get all, and more than all, at once. Observe, then, the language and the sufficiency of the promise.

But I want you to notice, further, *the continued freshness and force of the promise.* Somebody here owes another person fifty pounds, and he gives him a note of hand, " I promise to pay you fifty pounds." Very well! the man calls with that note of hand to-morrow, and gets fifty pounds. And what is the good of the note of hand now ? Why, it is of no further value, it is discharged. How would you like to have a note of hand which would always stand good? That would be a right royal present. "I promise to pay evermore, and this bond, though paid a thousand times, shall still hold good." Who would not like to have a cheque of that sort? Yet this is the promise which Christ gives you, "I will not leave you orphans: I will come to you." The first time a sinner looks to Christ, Christ comes to him. And what then? Why, the next minute it is still, "I will come to you." But here is one who has known Christ for fifty years, and he has had this promise fulfilled a thousand times a year: is it not done with? Oh, no! there it stands, just as fresh as when Jesus first spoke it, "I will come to you." Then we will treat our Lord in His own fashion, and take Him at His word. We will go to Him as often as ever we can, for we shall never weary Him; and when He has kept His promise most, then is it that we will go to Him, and ask Him to keep it more still; and after ten thousand proofs of the truth of it, we will only have a greater hungering and thirsting to get it fulfilled again. This is fit provision for life, and for death, "I will come to you." In the last moment, when your pulse beats faintly, and you are just about to pass the curtain, and enter into the invisible world, you may have this upon your lips, and say to your Lord, "My Master, still fulfil the word on which Thou hast caused me to hope, 'I will not leave you comfortless: I will come to you.'"

Let me remind you that *the text is at this moment valid*, and for this I delight in it. "I will not leave you comfortless." That means now, "I will not leave you comfortless *now*." Are you comfortless at this hour? It is your own fault. Jesus Christ does not leave you so, nor make you so. There are rich and precious things in this word, "I will not leave you comfortless: I will come to you, I will come to you now." It may be a very dull time with you, and you are pining to come nearer to Christ. Very well, then plead the promise before the Lord. Plead the promise as you sit where you are : " Lord, Thou hast said Thou wilt come unto me; come unto me to-night." There are many reasons, believer, why you should plead thus. You want Him; you need Him; you require Him; therefore plead the promise, and expect its fulfilment. And oh! when He cometh, what a joy it is ; He is as a bridegroom coming out of his chamber with his garments fragrant with aloes and cassia! How well the oil of joy will perfume your heart! How soon will your sackcloth be put away, and the garments of gladness adorn you! With what joy of heart will your heavy soul begin to sing when Jesus Christ shall whisper that you are His, and that He is yours! Come, my Beloved, make no tarrying; be Thou like a roe or a young hart upon the mountains of separation, and prove to me Thy promise true, "I will not leave you orphans: I will come to you."

And now, dear friends, in conclusion, let me remind you that *there are many who have no share in the text.* What can I say to such ? From my soul I pity you who do not know what the love of Christ means. Oh! if you could but tell the joy of God's people, you would not rest an hour without it.

> " His worth, if all the nations knew,
> Sure the whole world would love Him too."

Remember, if you would find Christ, He is to be found in the way of faith. Trust Him, and He is yours. Depend upon the merit of His sacrifice ; cast yourselves entirely upon that, and you are saved, and Christ is yours.

God grant that we may all break bread in the kingdom above, and feast with Jesus, and share His glory ! We are expecting His second coming. He is coming personally and gloriously. This is the brightest hope of His people. This will be the fulness of their redemption, the time of their resurrection. Anticipate it, beloved, and may God make your souls to sing for joy!

> " 'Mid the splendours of the glory
>   Which we hope ere long to share ;
>   Christ our Head, and we His members,
>   Shall appear, divinely fair.
>   Oh, how glorious !
>   When we meet Him in the air !
>
> " Bright the prospect soon that greets us
>   Of that long'd-for nuptial day,
>   When our heavenly Bridegroom meets us
>   On His kingly, conquering way ;
>   In the glory,
>   Bride and Bridegroom reign for aye !"

" Thou hast visited me in the night."—*Psalm* xvii. 3.

9

Mysterious Visits

IT is a theme for wonder that the glorious God should visit sinful man. "What is man, that Thou art mindful of him? and the son of man, that Thou visitest him?" A divine visit is a joy to be treasured whenever we are favoured with it. David speaks of it with great solemnity. The Psalmist was not content barely to *speak* of it; but he wrote it down in plain terms, that it might be known throughout all generations: "*Thou hast visited me in the night.*" Beloved, if God has ever visited you, you also will marvel at it, will carry it in your memory, will speak of it to your friends, and will record it in your diary as one of the notable events of your life. Above all, you will speak of it to God Himself, and say with adoring gratitude, "Thou hast visited me in the night." It should be a solemn part of worship to remember and make known the condescension of the Lord, and say, both in lowly prayer and in joyful psalm, "Thou hast visited me."

To you, beloved friends, who gather with me about this communion table, I will speak of my own experience, nothing doubting that it is also yours. If our God has ever visited any of us, personally, by His Spirit, two results have attended the visit: *it has been sharply searching*, and *it has been sweetly solacing*.

When first of all the Lord draws nigh to the heart,

the trembling soul perceives clearly the searching character of His visit. Remember how Job answered the Lord: " I have heard of Thee by the hearing of the ear : but now mine eye seeth Thee, wherefore I abhor myself, and repent in dust and ashes." We can read of God, and hear of God, and be little moved ; but when we feel His presence, it is another matter. I thought my house was good enough for kings ; but when the King of kings came to it, I saw that it was a hovel quite unfit for His abode. I had never known sin to be so "exceeding sinful" if I had not known God to be so perfectly holy. I had never understood the depravity of my own nature if I had not known the holiness of God's nature. When we see Jesus, we fall at His feet as dead ; till then, we are alive with vainglorious life. If letters of light traced by a mysterious hand upon the wall caused the joints of Belshazzar's loins to be loosed, what awe overcomes our spirits when we see the Lord Himself! In the presence of so much light our spots and wrinkles are revealed, and we are utterly ashamed. We are like Daniel, who said, " I was left alone, and saw this great vision, and there remained no strength in me : for my comeliness was turned in me into corruption." It is when the Lord visits us that we see our nothingness, and ask, " Lord, what is man ? "

I do remember well when God first visited me ; and assuredly it was the night of nature, of ignorance, of sin. His visit had the same effect upon me that it had upon Saul of Tarsus when the Lord spake to him out of heaven. He brought me down from the high horse, and caused me to fall to the ground ; by the brightness of the light of His Spirit He made me

grope in conscious blindness ; and in the brokenness
of my heart I cried, " Lord, what wilt Thou have me
to do ? " I felt that I had been rebelling against the
Lord, kicking against the pricks, and doing evil even
as I could ; and my soul was filled with anguish at
the discovery. Very searching was the glance of the
eye of Jesus, for it revealed my sin, and caused me to
go out and weep bitterly. As when the Lord visited
Adam, and called him to stand naked before Him, so
was I stripped of all my righteousness before the face
of the Most High. Yet the visit ended not there ; for
as the Lord God clothed our first parents in coats of
skins, so did He cover me with the righteousness of
the great sacrifice, and He gave me songs in the night.
It was night, but the visit was no dream : in fact, I
there and then ceased to dream, and began to deal
with the reality of things.

I think you will remember that, when the Lord first
visited you in the night, it was with you as with Peter
when Jesus came to him. He had been toiling with
his net all the night, and nothing had come of it ; but
when the Lord Jesus came into his boat, and bade
him launch out into the deep, and let down his net
for a draught, he caught such a great multitude of
fishes that the boat began to sink. See ! the boat
goes down, down, till the water threatens to engulf it,
and Peter, and the fish, and all. Then Peter fell
down at Jesus' knees, and cried, " Depart from me ;
for I am a sinful man, O Lord ! " The presence of
Jesus was too much for him : his sense of unworthiness made him sink like his boat, and shrink away
from the Divine Lord. I remember that sensation
well ; for I was half inclined to cry with the demoniac

of Gadara, "What have I to do with Thee, Jesus, Thou Son of God most high?" That first discovery of His injured love was overpowering; its very hopefulness increased my anguish; for then I saw that I had slain the Lord who had come to save me. I saw that mine was the hand which made the hammer fall, and drove the nails that fastened the Redeemer's hands and feet to the cruel tree.

> " My conscience felt and own'd the guilt,
>   And plunged me in despair ;
>   I saw my sins His blood had spilt,
>   And help'd to nail Him there."

This is the sight which breeds repentance : " They shall look upon Him whom they have pierced, and mourn for Him." When the Lord visits us, He humbles us, removes all hardness from our hearts, and leads us to the Saviour's feet.

When the Lord first visited us in the night, it was very much with us as with John, when the Lord visited him in the isle that is called Patmos. He tells us, " And when I saw Him, I fell at His feet as dead." Yes, even when we begin to see that He has put away our sin, and removed our guilt by His death, we feel as if we could never look up again, because we have been so cruel to our best Friend. It is no wonder if we then say, " It is true that He has forgiven me; but I never can forgive myself. He makes me live, and I live in Him ; but at the thought of His goodness I fall at His feet as dead. Boasting is dead, self is dead, and all desire for anything beyond my Lord is dead also." Well does Cowper sing of—

> " That dear hour, that brought me to His foot,
>   And cut up all my follies by the root."

The process of destroying follies is more hopefully performed at Jesus' feet than anywhere else. Oh, that the Lord would come again to us as at the first, and like a consuming fire discover and destroy the dross which now alloys our gold! The word *visit* brings to us who travel the remembrance of the government officer who searches our baggage ; thus doth the Lord seek out our secret things. But it also reminds us of the visits of the physician, who not only finds out our maladies, but also removes them. Thus did the Lord Jesus visit us at the first.

Since those early days, I hope that you and I have had many visits from our Lord. Those first visits were, as I said, sharply searching ; but the later ones have been *sweetly solacing*. Some of us have had them, especially in the night, when we have been compelled to count the sleepless hours. " Heaven's gate opens when this world's is shut." The night is still ; everybody is away ; work is done ; care is for-gotten, and then the Lord Himself draws near. Possibly there may be pain to be endured, the head may be aching, and the heart may be throbbing ; but if Jesus comes to visit us, our bed of languishing becomes a throne of glory. Though it is true " He giveth His beloved sleep," yet at such times He gives them some-thing better than sleep, namely, His own presence, and the fulness of joy which comes with it. By night upon our bed we have seen the unseen. I have tried some-times not to sleep under an excess of joy, when the company of Christ has been sweetly mine.

" Thou hast visited me in the night." Believe me, there are such things as personal visits from Jesus to His people. He has not left us utterly. Though He be not seen with the bodily eye by bush or brook, nor on the mount, nor by the sea, yet doth He come and go, observed only by the spirit, felt only by the heart. Still he standeth behind our wall, He showeth Himself through the lattices.

> " Jesus, these eyes have never seen
>   That radiant form of Thine !
> The veil of sense hangs dark between
>   Thy blessed face and mine !
>
> " I see Thee not, I hear Thee not,
>   Yet art Thou oft with me,
> And earth hath ne'er so dear a spot
>   As where I meet with Thee.
>
> " Like some bright dream that comes unsought,
>   When slumbers o'er me roll,
> Thine image ever fills my thought,
>   And charms my ravish'd soul.
>
> " Yet though I have not seen, and still
>   Must rest in faith alone ;
> I love Thee, dearest Lord ! and will,
>   Unseen, but not unknown."

Do you ask me to describe these manifestations of the Lord ? It were hard to tell you in words : you must know them for yourselves. If you had never tasted sweetness, no man living could give you an idea of honey. Yet if the honey be there, you can " taste and see." To a man born blind, sight must be a thing past imagination ; and to one who has never known the Lord, His visits are quite as much beyond conception.

For our Lord to visit us is something more than for us to have the assurance of our salvation, though that is very delightful, and none of us should rest satisfied unless we possess it. To know that Jesus loves me, is one thing; but to be visited by Him in love, is more.

Nor is it simply a close contemplation of Christ; for we can picture Him as exceedingly fair and majestic, and yet not have Him consciously near us. Delightful and instructive as it is to behold the likeness of Christ by meditation, yet the enjoyment of His actual presence is something more. I may wear my friend's portrait about my person, and yet may not be able to say, "Thou hast visited me."

It is the actual, though spiritual, coming of Christ which we so much desire. The Romish church says much about the *real* presence; meaning thereby, the corporeal presence of the Lord Jesus. The priest who celebrates mass tells us that he believes in the *real* presence, but we reply, "Nay, you believe in knowing Christ after the flesh, and in that sense the only real presence is in heaven; but we firmly believe in the real presence of Christ which is spiritual, and yet certain." By spiritual we do not mean unreal; in fact, the spiritual takes the lead in real-ness to spiritual men. I believe in the true and real presence of Jesus with His people: such presence has been real to my spirit. Lord Jesus, Thou Thyself hast visited me. As surely as the Lord Jesus came really as to His flesh to Bethlehem and Calvary, so surely does He come really by His Spirit to His people in the hours of their communion with Him. We are as conscious of that presence as of our own existence.

When the Lord visits us in the night, what is the effect upon us? When hearts meet hearts in fellowship of love, communion brings first peace, then rest, and then joy of soul. I am speaking of no emotional excitement rising into fanatical rapture ; but I speak of sober fact, when I say that the Lord's great heart touches ours, and our heart rises into sympathy with Him.

First, we experience *peace*. All war is over, and a blessed peace is proclaimed ; the peace of God keeps our heart and mind by Christ Jesus.

> " Peace ! perfect peace ! in this dark world of sin ?
> The blood of Jesus whispers peace within.

> " Peace ! perfect peace ! with sorrows surging round ?
> On Jesus' bosom nought but calm is found."

At such a time there is a delightful sense of *rest ;* we have no ambitions, no desires. A divine serenity and security envelop us. We have no thought of foes, or fears, or afflictions, or doubts. There is a joyous laying aside of our own will. We *are* nothing, and we *will* nothing : Christ is everything, and His will is the pulse of our soul. We are perfectly content either to be ill or to be well, to be rich or to be poor, to be slandered or to be honoured, so that we may but abide in the love of Christ. Jesus fills the horizon of our being.

At such a time a flood of great *joy* will fill our minds. We shall half wish that the morning may never break again, for fear its light should banish the superior light of Christ's presence. We shall wish that we could glide away with our Beloved to the place where He feedeth among the lilies. We long to hear the voices of the white-robed armies, that we may follow their glorious Leader whithersoever He goeth. I am persuaded that there is no great actual distance between earth and heaven : the distance lies in our dull minds. When the Beloved visits us in the night, He makes our chambers to be the vestibule of His palace-halls. Earth rises to heaven when heaven comes down to earth.

Now, beloved friends, you may be saying to yourselves, " *We* have not enjoyed such visits as these." You may do so. If the Father loves you even as He loves His Son, then you are on visiting terms with Him. If, then, He has not called upon you, you will be wise to call on Him. Breathe a sigh to Him, and say,—

> " When wilt Thou come unto me, Lord ?
>   Oh come, my Lord most dear !
> Come near, come nearer, nearer still,
>   I'm blest when Thou art near.
>
> " When wilt Thou come unto me, Lord ?
>   I languish for the sight ;
> Ten thousand suns when Thou art hid,
>   Are shades instead of light.
>
> " When wilt Thou come unto me, Lord ?
>   Until Thou dost appear,
> I count each moment for a day,
>   Each minute for a year."

" As the hart panteth after the water-brooks, so panteth my soul after Thee, O God ! " If you long for Him, He much more longs for you. Never was there a sinner that was half so eager for Christ as Christ is eager for the sinner ; nor a saint one-tenth so anxious to behold his Lord as his Lord is to behold him. If thou art running to Christ, He is already near thee. If thou dost sigh for His presence, that sigh is the evidence that He is with thee. He is with thee now : therefore be calmly glad.

Go forth, beloved, and talk with Jesus on the beach, for He oft resorted to the sea-shore. Commune with Him amid the olive-groves so dear to Him in many a night of wrestling prayer. If ever there was a country in which men should see traces of Jesus, next to the Holy Land, this Riviera is the favoured spot. It is a land of vines, and figs, and olives, and palms ; I have called it " Thy land, O Immanuel." While in this Mentone, I often fancy that I am looking out upon the Lake of Gennesaret, or walking at the foot of the Mount of Olives, or peering into the mysterious gloom of the Garden of Gethsemane. The narrow streets of the old town are such as Jesus traversed, these villages are such as He inhabited. Have your hearts right with Him, and He will visit you often, until every day you shall walk with God, as Enoch did, and so turn week-days into Sabbaths, meals into sacraments, homes into temples, and earth into heaven. So be it with us ! Amen.

"My Beloved is mine, and I am His : He feedeth among the lilies. Until the day break, and the shadows flee away, turn, my Beloved, and be Thou like a roe or a young hart upon the mountains of Bether."—*Solomon's Song* ii. **16, 17.**

10

Over the Mountains

IT may be that there are saints who are always at
their best, and are happy enough never to lose
the light of their Father's countenance. I am not
sure that there are such persons, for those believers
with whom I have been most intimate have had a
varied experience ; and those whom I have known,
who have boasted of their constant perfectness, have
not been the most reliable of individuals. I hope
there is a spiritual region attainable where there are
no clouds to hide the Sun of our soul ; but I cannot
speak with positiveness, for I have not traversed that
happy land. Every year of my life has had a winter
as well as a summer, and every day its night. I have
hitherto seen clear shinings and heavy rains, and felt
warm breezes and fierce winds. Speaking for the
many of my brethren, I confess that though the
substance be in us, as in the teil-tree and the oak, yet
we do lose our leaves, and the sap within us does not
flow with equal vigour at all seasons. We have our
downs as well as our ups, our valleys as well as our
hills. We are not always rejoicing ; we are sometimes in heaviness through manifold trials. Alas! we
are grieved to confess that our fellowship with the
Well-beloved is not always that of rapturous delight ;
but we have at times to seek Him, and cry, " Oh, that
I knew where I might find Him!" This appears to

me to have been in a measure the condition of the spouse when she cried, " Until the day break, and the shadows flee away, turn, my Beloved."

I. These words teach us, first, that COMMUNION MAY BE BROKEN. The spouse had lost the company of her Bridegroom : conscious communion with Him was gone, though she loved her Lord, and sighed for Him. In her loneliness she was sorrowful ; but *she had by no means ceased to love Him,* for she calls Him her Beloved, and speaks as one who felt no doubt upon that point. Love to the Lord Jesus may be quite as true, and perhaps quite as strong, when we sit in darkness as when we walk in the light. Nay, *she had not lost her assurance of His love to her,* and of their mutual interest in one another ; for she says, " My Beloved is mine, and I am His ; " and yet she adds, " Turn, my Beloved." The condition of our graces does not always coincide with the state of our joys. We may be rich in faith and love, and yet have so low an esteem of ourselves as to be much depressed.

It is plain, from this Sacred Canticle, that the spouse may love and be loved, may be confident in her Lord, and be fully assured of her possession of Him, and yet there may for the present be mountains between her and Him. Yes, we may even be far advanced in the divine life, and yet be exiled for a while from conscious fellowship. There are nights for men as well as babes, and the strong know that the sun is hidden quite as well as do the sick and the feeble. Do not, therefore, condemn yourself, my brother, because a cloud is over you ; cast not away your confidence ; but the rather let faith burn up in the gloom, and let your love resolve to come at your

Lord again whatever be the barriers which divide you from Him.

When Jesus is absent from a true heir of heaven, sorrow will ensue. The healthier our condition, the sooner will that absence be perceived, and the more deeply will it be lamented. This sorrow is described in the text as darkness; this is implied in the expression, "*Until the day break.*" Till Christ appears, no day has dawned for us. We dwell in midnight darkness; the stars of the promises and the moon of experience yield no light of comfort till our Lord, like the sun, arises and ends the night. We must have Christ with us, or we are benighted: we grope like blind men for the wall, and wander in dismay.

The spouse also speaks of shadows. "Until the day break, *and the shadows flee away.*" Shadows are multiplied by the departure of the sun, and these are apt to distress the timid. We are not afraid of real enemies when Jesus is with us; but when we miss Him, we tremble at a shade. How sweet is that song, "Yea, though I walk through the valley of the shadow of death, I will fear no evil: for Thou art with me; Thy rod and Thy staff they comfort me!" But we change our note when midnight is now come, and Jesus is not with us: then we people the night with terrors: spectres, demons, hobgoblins, and things that never existed save in fancy, are apt to swarm about us; and we are in fear where no fear is.

The spouse's worst trouble was that *the back of her Beloved was turned to her*, and so she cried, "Turn, my Beloved." When His face is towards her, she suns herself in His love; but if the light of His countenance

145

is withdrawn, she is sorely troubled. Our Lord turns His face from His people though He never turns His heart from His people. He may even close His eyes in sleep when the vessel is tossed by the tempest, but His heart is awake all the while. Still, it is pain enough to have grieved Him in any degree : it cuts us to the quick to think that we have wounded His tender heart. He is jealous, but never without cause. If He turns His back upon us for a while, He has doubtless a more than sufficient reason. He would not walk contrary to us if we had not walked contrary to Him. Ah, it is sad work this! The presence of the Lord makes this life the preface to the life celestial ; but His absence leaves us pining and fainting, neither doth any comfort remain in the land of our banishment. The Scriptures and the ordinances, private devotion and public worship, are all as sun-dials,—most excellent when the sun shines, but of small avail in the dark. O Lord Jesus, nothing can compensate us for Thy loss! Draw near to Thy beloved yet again, for without Thee our night will never end.

> "See ! I repent, and vex my soul,
> That I should leave Thee so !
> Where will those vile affections roll
> That let my Saviour go ?"

When communion with Christ is broken, in all true hearts *there is a strong desire to win it back again.* The man who has known the joy of communion with Christ, if he loses it, will never be content until it is restored. Hast thou ever entertained the Prince Emmanuel ? Is He gone elsewhere ? Thy chamber will be dreary till He comes back again. "Give me

Christ or else I die," is the cry of every spirit that has lost the dear companionship of Jesus. We do not part with such heavenly delights without many a pang. It is not with us a matter of " maybe He will return, and we hope He will ; " but it must be, or we faint and die. We cannot live without Him ; and this is a cheering sign ; for the soul that cannot live without Him shall not live without Him : He comes speedily where life and death hang on His coming. If you must have Christ you shall have Him. This is just how the matter stands : we must drink of this well or die of thirst ; we must feed upon Jesus or our spirit will famish.

II. We will now advance a step, and say that when communion with Christ is broken, THERE ARE GREAT DIFFICULTIES IN THE WAY OF ITS RENEWAL. It is much easier to go down hill than to climb to the same height again. It is far easier to lose joy in God than to find the lost jewel. The spouse speaks of " mountains " dividing her from her Beloved : she means that *the difficulties were great*. They were not little hills, but mountains, that closed up her way. Mountains of remembered sin, Alps of backsliding, dread ranges of forgetfulness, ingratitude, worldliness, coldness in prayer, frivolity, pride, unbelief. Ah me, I cannot teach you all the dark geography of this sad experience ! Giant walls rose before her like the towering steeps of Lebanon. How could she come at her Beloved ?

The dividing difficulties were many as well as great. She does not speak of " a mountain ", but of " mountains " : Alps rose on Alps, wall after wall. She was distressed to think that in so short a time so

147

much could come between her and Him of whom she sang just now, " His left hand is under my head, and His right hand doth embrace me." Alas, we multiply these mountains of Bether with a sad rapidity! Our Lord is jealous, and we give Him far too much reason for hiding His face. A fault, which seemed so small at the time we committed it, is seen in the light of its own consequences, and then it grows and swells till it towers aloft, and hides the face of the Beloved. Then has our sun gone down, and fear whispers, " Will His light ever return ? Will it ever be day-break ? Will the shadows ever flee away ? " It is easy to grieve away the heavenly sunlight, but ah, how hard to clear the skies, and regain the unclouded brightness !

Perhaps the worst thought of all to the spouse was the dread that *the dividing barrier might be permanent*. It was high, but it might dissolve ; the walls were many, but they might fall ; but, alas, they were mountains, and these stand fast for ages ! She felt like the Psalmist, when he cried, " My sin is ever before me." The pain of our Lord's absence becomes intolerable when we fear that we are hopelessly shut out from Him. A night one can bear, hoping for the morning ; but what if the day should never break ? And you and I, if we have wandered away from Christ, and feel that there are ranges of immovable mountains between Him and us, will feel sick at heart. We try to pray, but devotion dies on our lips. We attempt to approach the Lord at the communion-table, but we feel more like Judas than John. At such times we have felt that we would give our eyes once more to behold the Bridegroom's face, and to know that He delights in us as in happier days. Still there stand the awful mountains, black, threatening, impassable ; and in the far-off land the Life of our life is away, and grieved.

So the spouse seems to have come to the conclusion that *the difficulties in her way were insurmountable by her own power*. She does not even think of herself going over the mountains to her Beloved, but she cries, " Until the day break, and the shadows flee away, turn, my Beloved, and be Thou like a roe or a young hart upon the mountains of Bether." She will not try to climb the mountains, she knows she cannot : if they had been less high, she might have attempted it ; but their summits reach to heaven. If they had been less craggy or difficult, she might have tried to scale them ; but these mountains are terrible, and no foot may stand upon their lone crags. Oh, the mercy of utter self-despair ! I love to see a soul driven into that close corner, and forced therefore to look to God alone. The end of the creature is the beginning of the Creator. Where the sinner ends the Saviour begins. If the mountains can be climbed, we shall have to climb them ; but if they are quite impassable, then the soul cries out with the prophet, " Oh, that Thou wouldest rend the heavens, that Thou wouldest come down, that the mountains might flow down at Thy presence. As when the melting fire burneth, the fire causeth the waters to boil, to make Thy name known to Thine adversaries, that the nations may tremble at Thy presence. When Thou didst terrible things which we looked not for, Thou camest down, the mountains flowed down at Thy presence." Our souls are lame, they cannot move to Christ, and lo !

149

we turn our strong desires to Him, and fix our hopes alone upon Him ; will He not remember us in love, and fly to us as He did to His servant of old when He rode upon a cherub, and did fly, yea, He did fly upon the wings of the wind ?

III. Here arises THAT PRAYER OF THE TEXT WHICH FULLY MEETS THE CASE. "Turn, my Beloved, and be Thou like a roe or a young hart upon the mountains of division." Jesus can come to us when we cannot go to Him. The roe and the young hart, or, as you may read it, the gazelle and the ibex, live among the crags of the mountains, and leap across the abyss with amazing agility. For swiftness and sure-footedness they are unrivalled. The sacred poet said, " He maketh my feet like hinds' feet, and setteth me upon my high places," alluding to the feet of those creatures which are so fitted to stand securely on the mountain's side. Our blessed Lord is called, in the title of the twenty-second Psalm, "the Hind of the morning " ; and the spouse in this golden Canticle sings, " My Beloved is like a roe or a young hart ; behold He cometh, leaping upon the mountains, skipping upon the hills."

Here I would remind you that this prayer is one that we may fairly offer, because *it is the way of Christ to come to us* when our coming to Him is out of the question. "How ? " say you. I answer that of old He did this ; for we remember " His great love wherewith He loved us even when we were dead in trespasses and in sins." His first coming into the world in human form, was it not because man could never come to God until God had come to him ? I hear of no tears, or prayers, or entreaties after God on the part of our first parents; but the offended Lord spontaneously gave the promise that the Seed of the woman should bruise the serpent's head. Our Lord's coming into the world was unbought, unsought, unthought of; he came altogether of His own free will, delighting to redeem.

> "With pitying eyes, the Prince of grace
>   Beheld our helpless grief;
>   He saw, and (oh, amazing love!)
>   He ran to our relief."

His incarnation was a type of the way in which He comes to us by His Spirit. He saw us cast out, polluted, shameful, perishing; and as He passed by, His tender lips said, "Live!" In us is fulfilled that word, "I am found of them that sought Me not." We were too averse to holiness, too much in bondage to sin, ever to have returned to Him if He had not turned to us. What think you? Did He come to us when we were enemies, and will He not visit us now that we are friends? Did He come to us when we were dead sinners, and will He not hear us now that we are weeping saints? If Christ's coming to the earth was after this manner, and if His coming to each one of us was after this style, we may well hope that now He will come to us in like fashion, like the dew which refreshes the grass, and waiteth not for man, neither tarrieth for the sons of men. Besides, He is coming again in person, in the latter-day, and mountains of sin, and error, and idolatry, and superstition, and oppression stand in the way of His kingdom; but He will surely come and overturn, and overturn, till He shall reign over all. He will come in the latter-days, I say, though He shall leap the hills

151

to do it, and because of that I am sure we may comfortably conclude that He will draw near to us who mourn His absence so bitterly. Then let us bow our heads a moment, and silently present to His most excellent Majesty the petition of our text: "Turn, my Beloved, and be Thou like a roe or a young hart upon the mountains of division."

Our text gives us sweet assurance that *our Lord is at home with those difficulties* which are quite insurmountable by us. Just as the roe or the young hart knows the passes of the mountains, and the stepping-places among the rugged rocks, and is void of all fear among the ravines and the precipices, so does our Lord know the heights and depths, the torrents and the caverns of our sin and sorrow. He carried the whole of our transgression, and so became aware of the tremendous load of our guilt. He is quite at home with the infirmities of our nature; He knew temptation in the wilderness, heart-break in the garden, desertion on the cross. He is quite at home with pain and weakness, for "Himself took our infirmities, and bare our sicknesses." He is at home with despondency, for He was "a Man of sorrows, and acquainted with grief." He is at home even with death, for He gave up the ghost, and passed through the sepulchre to resurrection. O yawning gulfs and frowning steeps of woe, our Beloved, like hind or hart, has traversed your glooms! O my Lord, Thou knowest all that divides me from Thee; and Thou knowest also that I am far too feeble to climb these dividing mountains, so that I may come at Thee; therefore, I pray Thee, come Thou over the mountains to meet my longing spirit! Thou knowest each yawning gulf and slippery steep, but none of these can stay Thee; haste Thou to me, Thy servant, Thy beloved, and let me again live by Thy presence.

It is easy, too, for Christ to come over the mountains for our relief. It is easy for the gazelle to cross the mountains, it is made for that end; so is it easy for Jesus, for to this purpose was He ordained from of old that He might come to man in his worst estate, and bring with Him the Father's love. What is it that separates us from Christ? Is it a sense of sin? You have been pardoned once, and Jesus can renew most vividly a sense of full forgiveness. But you say, "Alas! I have sinned again: fresh guilt alarms me." He can remove it in an instant, for the fountain appointed for that purpose is opened, and is still full. It is easy for the dear lips of redeeming love to put away the child's offences, since He has already obtained pardon for the criminal's iniquities. If with His heart's blood He won our pardon from our Judge, he can easily enough bring us the forgiveness of our Father. Oh, yes, it is easy enough for Christ to say again, "Thy sins be forgiven"! "But I feel so unfit, so unable to enjoy communion." He that healed all manner of bodily diseases can heal with a word your spiritual infirmities. Remember the man whose ankle-bones received strength, so that he ran and leaped; and her who was sick of a fever, and was healed at once, and arose, and ministered unto her Lord. "My grace is sufficient for thee; for My strength is made perfect in weakness." "But I have such afflictions, such troubles, such sorrows, that I am weighted down, and cannot rise into joyful fellowship." Yes, but Jesus can make every burden light, and cause each yoke to be easy. Your trials can be made to aid your heavenward course instead of hindering it. I know all about those heavy weights, and I perceive that you cannot lift them ; but skilful engineers can adapt ropes and pulleys in such a way that heavy weights lift other weights. The Lord Jesus is great at gracious machinery, and He has the art of causing a weight of tribulation to lift from us a load of spiritual deadness, so that we ascend by that which, like a millstone, threatened to sink us down.

What else doth hinder ? I am sure that, if it were a sheer impossibility, the Lord Jesus could remove it, for things impossible with men are possible with God. But someone objects, "I am so unworthy of Christ. I can understand eminent saints and beloved disciples being greatly indulged, but I am a worm, and no man ; utterly below such condescension." Say you so ? Know you not that the worthiness of Christ covers your unworthiness, and He is made of God unto you wisdom, righteousness, sanctification, and redemption ? In Christ, the Father thinks not so meanly of you as you think of yourself ; you are not worthy to be called His child, but He does call you so, and reckons you to be among His jewels. Listen, and you shall hear Him say, "Since thou wast precious in My sight, thou hast been honourable, and I have loved thee. I gave Egypt for thy ransom ; Ethiopia and Seba for thee." Thus, then, there remains nothing which Jesus cannot overleap if He resolves to come to you, and re-establish your broken fellowship.

To conclude, *our Lord can do all this directly*. As in the twinkling of an eye the dead shall be raised incorruptible, so in a moment can our dead affections rise to fulness of delight. He can say to this mountain, " Be thou removed hence, and be thou cast into the midst of the sea," and it shall be done. In the sacred emblems now upon this supper table, Jesus is already among us. Faith cries, " He has come!" Like John the Baptist, she gazes intently on Him, and cries, " Behold the Lamb of God!" At this table Jesus feeds us with His body and His blood. His corporeal presence we have not, but His real spiritual presence we perceive. We are like the disciples when none of them durst ask Him, " Who art Thou?" knowing that it was the Lord. He is come. He looketh forth at these windows,—I mean this bread and wine; showing Himself through the lattices of this instructive and endearing ordinance. He speaks. He saith, " The winter is past, the rain is over and gone." And so it is; we feel it to be so: a heavenly springtide warms our frozen hearts. Like the spouse, we wonderingly cry, " Or ever I was aware, my soul made me like the chariots of Ammi-nadib." Now in happy fellowship we see the Beloved, and hear His voice; our heart burns; our affections glow; we are happy, restful, brimming over with delight. The King has brought us into his banqueting-house, and His banner over us is love. It is good to be here!

Friends, we must now go our ways. A voice saith, " Arise, let us go hence." O Thou Lord of our hearts, go with us! Home will not be home without Thee. Life will not be life without Thee. Heaven itself would not be heaven if Thou wert absent. Abide with us. The world grows dark, the gloaming of time draws on. Abide with us, for it is toward evening.

Our years increase, and we near the night when dews fall cold and chill. A great future is all about us, the splendours of the last age are coming down ; and while we wait in solemn, awe-struck expectation, our heart continually cries within herself, " Until the day break, and the shadows flee away, turn, my Beloved, and be Thou like a roe or a young hart upon the mountains of division."

" Hasten, Lord ! the promised hour ;
Come in glory and in power ;
Still Thy foes are unsubdued ;
Nature sighs to be renew'd.
Time has nearly reach'd its sum,
All things with Thy bride say ' Come ;'
Jesus, whom all worlds adore,
Come and reign for evermore ! "

"I would cause Thee to drink of spiced wine of the juice of my pomegranate."— *Solomon's Song* viii. 2.

" And of His fulness have all we received, and grace for grace." *John* i. 16.

11

The Spiced Wine of the Pomegranate

THE immovable basis of communion having been laid of old in the eternal union which subsisted between Christ and His elect, it only needed a fitting occasion to manifest itself in active development. The Lord Jesus had for ever delighted Himself with the sons of men, and he ever stood prepared to reveal and communicate that delight to His people ; but they were incapable of returning His affection or enjoying His fellowship, having fallen into a state so base and degraded, that they were dead to Him, and careless concerning Him. It was therefore needful that something should be done for them, and in them, before they could hold converse with Jesus, or feel concord with Him. This preparation being a work of grace and a result of previous union, Jesus determined that, even in the preparation for communion, there should be communion. If they must be washed before they could fully converse with Him, He would commune with them in the washing ; and if they must be enriched by gifts before they could have full access to Him, He would commune with them in the giving. He has therefore established a fellowship in imparting His grace, and in partaking of it.

This order of fellowship we have called "The Communion of Communication," and we think that a few remarks will prove that we are not running beyond the warranty of Scripture.

The word κοινωνια, or communion, is frequently employed by inspired writers in the sense of communication or contribution. When, in our English version, we read, "For it hath pleased them of Macedonia and Achaia to make *a certain contribution* for the poor saints which are at Jerusalem" (Romans xv. 26), it is interesting to know that the word κοινωνιαν is used, as if to show that the generous gifts of the Church in Achaia to its sister Church at Jerusalem was a communion. Calvin would have us notice this, because, saith he, "The word here employed well expresses the feeling by which it behoves us to succour the wants of our brethren, even because there is to be a common and mutual regard on account of the union of the body." He would not have strained the text if he had said that there was in the contribution the very essence of communion. Gill, in his commentary upon the above verse, most pertinently remarks, "Contribution, or communion, as the word signifies, it being one part of the communion of churches and of saints to relieve their poor by communicating to them." The same word is employed in Hebrews xiii. 16, and is there translated by the word "*communicate.*" "But to do good, and to communicate, forget not: for with such sacrifices God is well pleased." It occurs again in 2 Corinthians ix. 13, "And for your liberal *distribution* unto them, and unto all men;" and in numerous other passages the careful student will observe the word in various forms, representing the ministering of the saints to one another as an act of fellowship. Indeed, at the Lord's supper, which is the embodiment of communion, we have ever been wont to make a special contribution for the poor of the flock, and we believe that in the collection there is as true and real an element of communion as in the partaking of the bread and wine. The giver holds fellowship with the receiver when he bestows his benefaction for the Lord's sake, and because of the brotherhood existing between him and his needy friends. The teacher holds communion with the young disciple when he labours to instruct him in the faith, being moved thereto by a spirit of Christian love. He who intercedes for a saint because he desires his well-being as a member of the one family, enters into fellowship with his brother in the offering of prayer. The loving and mutual service of church-members is fellowship of a high degree. And let us remember that the recipient communes with the benefactor: the communion is not confined to the giver, but the heart overflowing with liberality is met by the heart brimming with gratitude, and the love manifested in the bestowal is reciprocated in the acceptance. When the hand feeds the mouth or supports the head, the divers members feel their union, and sympathize with one another; and so is it with the various portions of the body of Christ, for they commune in mutual acts of love.

Now, this meaning of the word communion furnishes us with much instruction, since it indicates the manner in which recognized fellowship with Jesus is commenced and maintained, namely, by giving and receiving, by *communication* and reception. The Lord's supper is the divinely-ordained exhibition of communion, and therefore in it there is the breaking of bread and the pouring forth of wine, to picture the free gift of the Saviour's body and blood to us; and there is also the eating of the one and the drinking of the other, to represent the reception of these priceless gifts by us. As without bread and wine there could be no Lord's supper, so without the gracious bequests of Jesus to us there would have been no communion between Him and our souls: and as participation is necessary before the elements truly represent the meaning of the Lord's ordinance, so is it needful that we should receive His bounties, and feed upon His person, before we can commune with Him.

It is one branch of this mutual communication which we have selected as the subject of this address. "Looking unto Jesus," who hath delivered us from our state of enmity, and brought us into fellowship with Himself, we pray for the rich assistance of the Holy Spirit, that we may be refreshed in spirit, and encouraged to draw more largely from the covenant storehouse of Christ Jesus the Lord.

We shall take a text, and proceed at once to our delightful task. "*And of His fulness have all we received, and grace for grace.*" (John i. 16.)

As the life of grace is first begotten in us by the Lord Jesus, so is it constantly sustained by Him. We are always drawing from this sacred fountain, always deriving sap from this divine root; and as Jesus communes with us in the bestowing of mercies, it is our privilege to hold fellowship with Him in the receiving of them.

There is this difference between Christ and ourselves, He never gives without manifesting fellowship, but we often receive in so ill a manner that communion is not reciprocated, and we therefore miss the heavenly opportunity of its enjoyment. We frequently receive grace insensibly, that is to say, the sacred oil runs through the pipe, and maintains our lamp, while we are unmindful of the secret influence. We may also be the partakers of many mercies which, through our dulness, we do not perceive to be mercies at all ; and at other times well-known blessings are recognized as such, but we are backward in tracing them to their source in the covenant made with Christ Jesus.

Following out the suggestion of our explanatory preface, we can well believe that when the poor saints received the contribution of their brethren, many of them did in earnest acknowledge the fellowship which was illustrated in the generous offering, but it is probable that some of them merely looked upon the material of the gift, and failed to see the spirit moving in it. Sensual thoughts in some of the receivers might possibly, at the season when the contribution was distributed, have mischievously injured the exercise of spirituality, for it is possible that, after a period of poverty, they would be apt to give greater prominence to the fact that their need was removed than to the sentiment of fellowship with their sympathizing brethren. They would rather rejoice over famine averted than concerning fellowship manifested. We doubt not that, in many instances, the mutual benefactions of the Church fail to reveal our fellowship to our poor brethren, and produce in them no feelings of communion with the givers.

Now this sad fact is an illustration of the yet more lamentable statement which we have made. We again assert that, as many of the partakers of the alms of the Church are not alive to the communion contained therein, so the Lord's people are never

sufficiently attentive to fellowship with Jesus in
receiving His gifts, but many of them are entirely
forgetful of their privilege, and all of them are too
little aware of it. Nay, worse than this, how often
doth the believer pervert the gifts of Jesus into food
for his own sin and wantonness! We are not free
from the fickleness of ancient Israel, and well might
our Lord address us in the same language : " Now
when I passed by thee, and looked upon thee, behold,
thy time was the time of love ; and I spread My
skirt over thee, and covered thy nakedness : yea, I
sware unto thee, and entered into a covenant with
thee, saith the Lord God, and thou becamest Mine.
Then washed I thee with water ; yea, I throughly
washed away thy blood from thee, and I anointed thee
with oil. I clothed thee also with broidered work, and
shod thee with badgers' skin, and I girded thee
about with fine linen, and I covered thee with silk.
I decked thee also with ornaments, and I put bracelets
upon thy hands, and a chain on thy neck. And I put
a jewel on thy forehead, and earrings in thine ears,
and a beautiful crown upon thine head. Thus wast
thou decked with gold and silver ; and thy raiment was
of fine linen, and silk, and broidered work ; thou didst
eat fine flour, and honey, and oil : and thou wast exceeding beautiful, and thou didst prosper into a kingdom.
And thy renown went forth among the heathen for
thy beauty : for it was perfect through My comeliness,
which I had put upon thee, saith the Lord God. But
thou didst trust in thine own beauty, and playedst the
harlot because of thy renown." (Ezek. xvi. 8—16.)

Ought not the mass of professors to confess the
truth of this accusation ? Have not the bulk of us

most sadly departed from the purity of our love? We rejoice, however, to observe a remnant of choice spirits, who live near the Lord, and know the sweetness of fellowship. These receive the promise and the blessing, and so digest them that they become good blood in their veins, and so do they feed on their Lord that they grow up into Him. Let us imitate those elevated minds, and obtain their high delights. There is no reason why the meanest of us should not be as David, and David as the servant of the Lord. We may now be dwarfs, but growth is possible; let us therefore aim at a higher stature. Let the succeeding advice be followed, and, the Holy Spirit helping us, we shall have attained thereto.

Make every time of need a time of embracing thy Lord. Do not leave the mercy-seat until thou hast clasped Him in thine arms. In every time of need He has promised to give thee grace to help, and what withholdeth thee from obtaining sweet fellowship as a precious addition to the promised assistance? Be not as the beggar who is content with the alms, however grudgingly it may be cast to him; but, since thou art a near kinsman, seek a smile and a kiss with every benison He gives thee. Is He not better than His mercies? What are they without Him? Cry aloud unto Him, and let thy petition reach His ears, "O my Lord, it is not enough to be a partaker of Thy bounties, I must have Thyself also; if Thou dost not give me Thyself with Thy favours, they are but of little use to me! O smile on me, when Thou blessest me, for else I am still unblest! Thou puttest perfume into all the flowers of Thy garden, and fragrance into Thy spices; if Thou withdrawest Thyself, they are no more pleasant to me. Come, then, my Lord, and give me Thy love with Thy grace." Take good heed, Christian, that thine own heart is in right tune, that when the fingers of mercy touch the strings, they may resound with full notes of communion. How sad is it to partake of favour without rejoicing in it! Yet such is often the believer's case. The Lord casts His lavish bounties at our doors, and we, like churls, scarcely look out to thank Him. Our ungrateful hearts and unthankful tongues mar our fellowship, by causing us to miss a thousand opportunities for exercising it.

If thou wouldst enjoy communion with the Lord Jesus in the reception of His grace, *endeavour to be always sensibly drawing supplies from Him.* Make thy needs public in the streets of thine heart, and when the supply is granted, let all the powers of thy soul be present at the reception of it. Let no mercy come into thine house unsung. Note in thy memory the list of thy Master's benefits. Wherefore should the Lord's bounties be hurried away in the dark, or buried in forgetfulness? Keep the gates of thy soul ever open, and sit thou by the wayside to watch the treasures of grace which God the Spirit hourly conveys into thy heart from Jehovah-Jesus, thy Lord.

Never let an hour pass without drawing upon the bank of heaven. If all thy wants seem satisfied, look steadfastly until the next moment brings another need, and then delay not, but with this warrant of necessity, hasten to thy treasury again. Thy necessities are so numerous that thou wilt never lack a reason for applying to the fulness of Jesus; but if ever such an occasion should arise, enlarge thine heart, and then there will be need of more love to fill the wider space.

But do not allow any supposititious riches of thine own to suspend thy daily receivings from the Lord Jesus. You have constant need of Him. You need His intercession, His upholding, His sanctification ; you need that He should work all your works in you, and that He should preserve you unto the day of His appearing. There is not one moment of your life in which you can do without Christ. Therefore be always at His door, and the wants which you bemoan shall be remembrances to turn your heart unto your Saviour. Thirst makes the heart pant for the water-brooks, and pain reminds man of the physician. Let your wants conduct you to Jesus, and may the blessed Spirit reveal Him unto you while He lovingly affords you the rich supplies of His love ! Go, poor saint, let thy poverty be the cord to draw thee to thy rich Brother. Rejoice in the infirmity which makes room for grace to rest upon thee, and be glad that thou hast constant needs which compel thee perpetually to hold fellowship with thine adorable Redeemer.

Study thyself, seek out thy necessities, as the housewife searches for chambers where she may bestow her summer fruits. Regard thy wants as rooms to be filled with more of the grace of Jesus, and suffer no corner to be unoccupied. Pant after more of Jesus. Be covetous after Him. Let all the past incite thee to seek greater things. Sing the song of the enlarged heart,—

> " All this is not enough : methinks I grow
>   More greedy by fruition ; what I get
>   Serves but to set
>   An edge upon my appetite ;
>   And all Thy gifts invite
>   My pray'rs for more."

Cry out to the Lord Jesus to fill the dry beds of thy rivers until they overflow, and then empty thou the channels which have hitherto been filled with thine own self-sufficiency, and beseech Him to fill these also with His superabundant grace. If thy heavy trials sink thee deeper in the flood of His consolations, be glad of them ; and if thy vessel shall be sunken up to its very bulwarks, be not afraid. I would be glad to feel the mast-head of my soul twenty fathoms beneath the surface of such an ocean ; for, as Rutherford said, " Oh, to be over the ears in this well ! I would not have Christ's love entering into me, but I would enter into it, and be swallowed up of that love." Cultivate an insatiable hunger and a quenchless thirst for this communion with Jesus through His communications. Let thine heart cry for ever, " Give, give," until it is filled in Paradise.

> " O'ercome with Jesu's condescending love,
> Brought into fellowship with Him and His,
> And feasting with Him in His house of wine,
> I'm sick of love,—and yet I pant for more
> Communications from my loving Lord.
> Stay me with flagons full of choicest wine,
> Press'd from His heart upon Mount Calvary,
> To cheer and comfort my love-conquer'd soul.
>   *   *   *   Thyself I crave !
> Thy presence is my life, my joy, my heav'n,
> And all, without Thyself, is dead to me.
> Stay me with flagons, Saviour, hear my cry,
> Let promises, like apples, comfort me ;
> Apply atoning blood, and cov'nant love,
> Until I see Thy face among the guests
> Who in Thy Father's kingdom feast."
>
>   (*Nymphas, by* JOSEPH IRONS.)

This is the only covetousness which is allowable : but

this is not merely beyond rebuke, it is worthy of commendation. O saints, be not straitened in your own bowels, but enlarge your desires, and so receive more of your Saviour's measureless fulness! I charge thee, my soul, thus to hold continual fellowship with thy Lord, since He invites and commands thee thus to partake of His riches.

Rejoice thyself in benefits received. Let the satisfaction of thy spirit overflow in streams of joy. When the believer reposes all his confidence in Christ, and delights himself in Him, there is an exercise of communion. If he forgetteth his psalm-book, and instead of singing is found lamenting, the mercies of the day will bring no communion. Awake, O music! stir up thyself, O my soul, be glad in the Lord, and exceedingly rejoice! Behold His favours, rich, free, and continual; shall they be buried in unthankfulness? Shall they be covered with a winding-sheet of ingratitude? No! I will praise Him. I must extol Him Sweet Lord Jesus, let me kiss the dust of Thy feet, let me lose myself in thankfulness, for Thy thoughts unto me are precious, how great is the sum of them! Lo, I embrace Thee in the arms of joy and gratitude, and herein I find my soul drawn unto Thee!

This is a blessed method of fellowship. It is kissing the divine lip of benediction with the sanctified lip of affection. Oh, for more rejoicing grace, more of the songs of the heart, more of the melody of the soul!

Seek to recognize the source of thy mercies as lying alone in Him who is our Head. Imitate the chicken, which, every time it drinketh of the brook, lifts up its head to heaven, as if it would return thanks for every drop. If we have anything that is commendable and gracious, it must come from the Holy Spirit, and that Spirit is first bestowed on Jesus, and then through Him on us. The oil was first poured on the head of Aaron, and thence it ran down upon his garments. Look on the drops of grace, and remember that they distil from the Head, Christ Jesus. All thy rays are begotten by this Sun of Righteousness, all thy showers are poured from this heaven, all thy fountains spring from this great and immeasurable depth. Oh, for grace to see the hand of Jesus on every favour! So will communion be constantly and firmly in exercise. May the great Teacher perpetually direct us to Jesus by making the mercies of the covenant the handposts on the road which leadeth to Him. Happy is the believer who knows how to find the secret abode of his Beloved by tracking the footsteps of His loving providence : herein is wisdom which the casual observer of mere second causes can never reach. Labour, O Christian, to follow up every clue which thy Master's grace affords thee !

Labour to maintain a sense of thine entire dependence upon His good will and pleasure for the continuance of thy richest enjoyments. Never try to live on the old manna, nor seek to find help in Egypt. All must come from Jesus, or thou art undone for ever. Old anointings will not suffice to impart unction to our spirit ; thine head must have fresh oil poured upon it from the golden horn of the sanctuary, or it will cease from its glory. To-day thou mayest be upon the summit of the mount of God ; but He who has put thee there must keep thee there, or thou wilt sink far more speedily than thou dreamest. Thy mountain only stands firm when He settles it in its place ; if He

170

hide His face, thou wilt soon be troubled. If the Saviour should see fit, there is not a window through which thou seest the light of heaven which he could not darken in an instant. Joshua bade the sun stand still, but Jesus can shroud it in total darkness. He can withdraw the joy of thine heart, the light of thine eyes, and the strength of thy life ; in His hand thy comforts lie, and at His will they can depart from thee. Oh ! how rich the grace which supplies us so continually, and doth not refrain itself because of our ingratitude ! O Lord Jesus, we would bow at Thy feet, conscious of our utter inability to do aught without Thee, and in every favour which we are privileged to receive, we would adore Thy blessed name, and acknowledge Thine unexhausted love !

When thou hast received much, admire the all-sufficiency which still remaineth undiminished, thus shall you commune with Christ, not only in what you obtain from Him, but also in the superabundance which remains treasured up in Him. Let us ever remember that giving does not impoverish our Lord. When the clouds, those wandering cisterns of the skies, have poured floods upon the dry ground, there remains an abundance in the storehouse of the rain : so in Christ there is ever an unbounded supply, though the most liberal showers of grace have fallen ever since the foundation of the earth. The sun is as bright as ever after all his shining, and the sea is quite as full after all the clouds have been drawn from it : so is our Lord Jesus ever the same overflowing fountain of fulness. All this is ours, and we may make it the subject of rejoicing fellowship. Come, believer, walk through the length and breadth of the land, for as far as the eye can reach, the land is thine, and far beyond the utmost range of thine observation it is thine also, the gracious gift of thy gracious Redeemer and Friend. Is there not ample space for fellowship *here?*

Regard every spiritual mercy as an assurance of the Lord's communion with thee. When the young man gives jewels to the virgin to whom he is affianced, she regards them as tokens of his delight in her. Believer, do the same with the precious presents of thy Lord. The common bounties of providence are shared in by all men, for the good Householder provides water for His swine as well as for His children : such things, therefore, are no proof of divine complacency. But thou hast richer food to eat ; " the children's bread " is in thy wallet, and the heritage of the righteous is reserved for thee. Look, then, on every motion of grace in thine heart as a pledge and sign of the moving of thy Saviour's heart towards thee. There is His whole heart in the bowels of every mercy which He sends thee. He has impressed a kiss of love upon each gift, and He would have thee believe that every jewel of mercy is a token of His boundless love. Look on thine adoption, justification, and preservation, as sweet enticements to fellowship. Let every note of the promise sound in thine ears like the ringing of the bells of the house of thy Lord, inviting thee to come to the banquets of His love. Joseph sent to his father asses laden with the good things of Egypt, and good old Jacob doubtless regarded them as pledges of the love of his son's heart : be sure not to think less of the kindnesses of Jesus.

Study to know the value of His favours. They are

no ordinary things, no paste jewels, no mosaic gold :
they are every one of them so costly, that, had all
heaven been drained of treasure, apart from the
precious offering of the Redeemer, it could not have
purchased so much as the least of His benefits.
When thou seest thy pardon, consider how great a
boon is contained in it! Bethink thee that hell had
been thine eternal portion unless Christ had plucked
thee from the burning! When thou art enabled to
see thyself as clothed in the imputed righteousness
of Jesus, admire the profusion of precious things of
which thy robe is made. Think how many times the
Man of sorrows wearied Himself at that loom of
obedience in which He wove that matchless garment;
and reckon, if thou canst, how many worlds of merit
were cast into the fabric at every throw of the shuttle!
Remember that all the angels in heaven could not
have afforded Him a single thread which would have
been rich enough to weave into the texture of His
perfect righteousness. Consider the cost of thy
maintenance for an hour; remember that thy wants
are so large, that all the granaries of grace that all the
saints could fill, could not feed thee for a moment.

What an expensive dependent thou art! King
Solomon made marvellous provision for his household
(1 Kings iv. 22), but all his beeves and fine flour
would be as the drop of the bucket compared with thy
daily wants. Rivers of oil, and ten thousand rams
or fed beasts, would not provide enough to supply
the necessities of thy hungering soul. Thy least
spiritual want demands infinity to satisfy it, and what
must be the amazing aggregate of thy perpetually-
repeated draughts upon thy Lord! Arise, then, and

bless thy loving Immanuel for the invaluable riches with which He has endowed thee. See what a dowry thy Bridegroom has brought to His poor, penniless spouse. He knows the value of the blessings which He brings thee, for He has paid for them out of His heart's richest blood ; be not thou so ungenerous as to pass them over as if they were but of little worth. Poor men know more of the value of money than those who have always revelled in abundance of wealth. Ought not thy former poverty to teach thee the preciousness of the grace which Jesus gives thee ? For remember, there was a time when thou wouldst have given a thousand worlds, if they had been thine, in order to procure the very least of His abundant mercies.

Remember how impossible it would have been for thee to receive a single spiritual blessing unless thou hadst been in Jesus. On none of Adam's race can the love of God be fixed, unless they are seen to be in union with His Son. No exception has ever been made to the universal curse on those of the first Adam's seed who have no interest in the second Adam. Christ is the only Zoar in which God's Lots can find a shelter from the destruction of Sodom. Out of Him, the withering blast of the fiery furnace of God's wrath consumes every green herb, and it is only in Him that the soul can live. As when the prairie is on fire, men see the heavens wrapped in sheets of flame, and in hot haste they fly before the devouring element. They have but one hope. There is in the distance a lake of water. They reach it, they plunge into it, and are safe. Although the skies are molten with the heat, the sun darkened with the smoke, and the earth utterly consumed in the fire, they know that they are secure while the cooling flood embraces them. Christ Jesus is the only escape for a sinner pursued by the fiery wrath of God, and we would have the believer remember this. Our own works could never shelter us, for they have proved but refuges of lies. Had they been a thousand times more and better, they would have been but as the spider's web, too frail to hang eternal interests upon. There was but one name, one sacrifice, one blood, by which we could escape. All other attempts at salvation were a grievous failure. For, " though a man could scourge out of his body rivers of blood, and in neglect of himself could outfast Moses or Elias; though he could wear out his knees with prayer, and had his eyes nailed on heaven; though he could build hospitals for all the poor on earth, and exhaust the mines of India in alms; though he could walk like an angel of light, and with the glittering of an outward holiness dazzle the eyes of all beholders; nay (if it were possible to be conceived) though he should live for a thousand years in a perfect and perpetual observation of the whole law of God, if the only exception to his perfection were the very least deviation from the law, yet such a man as this could no more appear before the tribunal of God's justice, than stubble before a consuming fire." * How, then, with thine innumerable sins, couldst thou escape the damnation of hell, much less become the recipient of bounties so rich and large? Blessed window of heaven, sweet Lord Jesus, let Thy Church for ever adore Thee, as the only channel by which

---

* Reynolds on the Life of Christ.

mercies can flow to her. My soul, give Him continual praise, for without Him thou hadst been poorer than a beggar. Be thou mindful, O heir of heaven, that thou couldst not have had one ray of hope, or one word of comfort, if thou hadst not been in union with Christ Jesus! The crumbs which fall from thy table are more than grace itself would have given thee, hadst thou not been in Jesus beloved and approved.

All thou hast, thou hast in Him : in Him chosen, in Him redeemed, in Him justified, in Him accepted. Thou art risen in Him, but without Him thou hadst died the second death. Thou art in Him raised up to the heavenly places, but out of Him thou wouldst have been damned eternally. Bless Him, then. Ask the angels to bless Him. Rouse all ages to a harmony of praise for His condescending love in taking poor guilty nothings into oneness with His all-adorable person. This is a blessed means of promoting communion, if the sacred Comforter is pleased to take of the things of Christ, and reveal them to us as ours, but only ours as we are in Him. Thrice-blessed Jesus, let us never forget that we are members of Thy mystical body, and that it is for this reason that we are blessed and preserved.

Meditate upon the gracious acts which procured thy blessings. Consider the ponderous labours which thy Lord endured for thee, and the stupendous sufferings by which He purchased the mercies which He bestows. What human tongue can speak forth the unutterable misery of His heart, or describe so much as one of the agonies which crowded upon His soul? How much less shall any finite comprehension arrive at an idea of the vast total of His woe! But all His sorrows were necessary for thy benefit, and without them not one of thine unnumbered mercies could have been bestowed. Be not unmindful that—

> " There's ne'er a gift His hand bestows,
> But cost His heart a groan."

Look upon the frozen ground of Gethsemane, and behold the bloody sweat which stained the soil! Turn to the hall of Gabbatha, and see the victim of justice pursued by His clamorous foes! Enter the guard-room of the Prætorians, and view the spitting, and the plucking of the hair! and then conclude your review upon Golgotha, the mount of doom, where death consummated His tortures ; and if, by divine assistance thou art enabled to enter, in some humble measure, into the depths of thy Lord's sufferings, thou wilt be the better prepared to hold fellowship with Him when next thou receivest His priceless gifts. In proportion to thy sense of their costliness will be thy capacity for enjoying the love which is centred in them.

Above all, and chief of all, never forget that Christ is thine. Amid the profusion of His gifts, never forget that the chief gift is Himself, and do not forget that, after all, His gifts are but Himself. He clothes thee, but it is with Himself, with His own spotless righteousness and character. He washes thee, but His innermost self, His own heart's blood, is the stream with which the fountain overflows. He feeds thee with the bread of heaven, but be not unmindful that the bread is Himself, His own body which He gives to be the food of souls. Never be satisfied with a less communication than a whole Christ. A wife will not be put off with maintenance, jewels, and attire, all these will be nothing to her unless she can call her husband's heart and person her own. It was the Paschal lamb upon which the ancient Israelite did feast on that night that was never to be forgotten. So do thou feast on Jesus, and on nothing less than Jesus, for less than this will be food too light for thy soul's satisfaction. Oh, be careful to eat His flesh and drink His blood, and so receive Him into thyself in a real and spiritual manner, for nothing short of this will be an evidence of eternal life in thy soul!

What more shall we add to the rules which we have here delivered? There remains but one great exhortation, which must not be omitted. *Seek the abundant assistance of the Holy Spirit* to enable you to put into practice the things which we have said, for without His aid, all that we have spoken will but be tantalizing the lame with rules to walk, or the dying with regulations for the preservation of health. O thou Divine Spirit, while we enjoy the grace of Jesus, lead us into the secret abode of our Lord, that we may sup with Him, and He with us, and grant unto us hourly grace that we may continue in the company of our Lord from the rising to the setting of the sun! Amen.

"I will give you rest."—*Matthew* xi. 28.

12

"I Will Give You Rest"

WE have a thousand times considered these words as an encouragement to the labouring and the laden ; and we may, therefore, have failed to read them as a promise to ourselves. But, beloved friends, we *have* come to Jesus, and therefore He stands engaged to fulfil this priceless pledge to us. We may now enjoy the promise; for we have obeyed the precept. The faithful and true Witness, whose word is truth, promised us rest if we would come to Him ; and, therefore, since we have come to Him, and are always coming to Him, we may boldly say, " O Thou, who art our Peace, make good Thy word to us wherein Thou hast said, I will give you rest.'"

By faith, I see our Lord standing in our midst, and I hear Him say, with voice of sweetest music, first to all of us together, and then to each one individually, " I will give you rest." May the Holy Spirit bring to each of us the fulness of the rest and peace of God! For a few minutes only shall I need your attention ; and we will begin by asking the question,—

I. WHAT MUST THESE WORDS MEAN ?

A dear friend prayed this morning that, while studying the Scriptures, we might be enabled to read between the lines, and beneath the letter of the Word. May we have holy insight thus to read our Lord's most gracious language !

This promise must mean rest to all parts of our spiritual nature. Our bodies cannot rest if the head is aching, or the feet are full of pain ; if one member is disturbed, the whole frame is unable to rest ; and so the higher nature is one, and such intimate sympathies bind together all its faculties and powers, that every one of them must rest, or none can be at ease. Jesus gives real, and, consequently, universal rest to every part of our spiritual being.

The heart is by nature restless as old ocean's waves ; it seeks an object for its affection ; and when it finds one beneath the stars, it is doomed to sorrow. Either the beloved changes, and there is disappointment ; or death comes in, and there is bereavement. The more tender the heart, the greater its unrest. Those in whom the heart is simply one of the largest valves are undisturbed, because they are callous ; but the sensitive, the generous, the unselfish, are often found seeking rest and finding none. To such, the Lord Jesus says, " Come unto Me, and I will give you rest." Look hither, ye loving ones, for here is a refuge for your wounded love ! You may delight yourselves in the Well-beloved, and never fear that He will fail or forget you. Love will not be wasted, however much it may be lavished upon Jesus. He deserves it all, and he requites it all. In loving Him, the heart finds a delicious content. When the head lies in His bosom, it enjoys an ease which no pillow of down could bestow. How Madame Guyon rested amid severe persecutions, because her great love to Jesus filled her soul to the brim ! O aching heart, O breaking heart, come hither, for Jesus saith, " I will give you rest."

The conscience, when it is at all alive and awake, is

much disturbed because the holy law of God has been broken by sin. Now, conscience once aroused is not easily quieted. Neither unbelief nor superstition can avail to lull it to sleep; it defies these opiates of falsehood, and frets the soul with perpetual annoyance. Like the troubled sea, it cannot rest; but constantly casts up upon the shore of memory the mire and dirt of past transgressions and iniquities. Is this your case? Then Jesus says, "I will give you rest." If, at any time, fears and apprehensions arise from an awakened conscience, they can only be safely and surely quieted by our flying to the Crucified. In the blessed truth of a substitution, accepted of God, and fully made by the Lord Jesus, our mind finds peace. Justice is honoured, and law is vindicated, in the sacrifice of Christ. Since God is satisfied, I may well be so. Since the Father has raised Jesus from the dead, and set Him at His own right hand, there can be no question as to His acceptance; and, consequently, all who are in Him are accepted also. We are under no apprehension now as to our being condemned; Jesus gives us rest, by enabling us to utter the challenge, "Who is he that condemneth?" and to give the reassuring answer, "Christ hath died."

The intellect is another source of unrest; and in these times it operates with special energy towards labour and travail of mind. Doubts, stinging like mosquitoes, are suggested by almost every page of the literature of the day. Most men are drifting, like vessels which have no anchors, and these come into collision with us. How can we rest? This scheme of philosophy eats up the other; this new fashion of heresy devours the last. Is there any foundation? Is anything true?

Or is it all romance, and are we doomed to be the victims of an ever-changing lie? O soul, seek not a settlement by learning of men; but come and learn of Jesus, and thou shalt find rest! Believe Jesus, and let all the Rabbis contradict. The Son of God was made flesh, He lived, He died, He rose again, He lives, He loves; this is true, and all that He teaches in His Word is assured verity; the rest may blow away, like chaff before the wind. A mind in pursuit of truth is a dove without a proper resting-place for the sole of its foot, till it finds its rest in Jesus, the true Noah.

Next, *these words mean rest about all things.* He who is uneasy about anything has not found rest. A thousand thorns and briars grow on the soil of this earth, and no man can happily tread life's ways unless his feet are shod with that preparation of the gospel of peace which Jesus gives. In Christ, we are at rest as to our duties; for He instructs and helps us in them. In Him, we are at rest about our trials; for He sympathizes with us in them. With His love, we are restful as to the movements of Providence; for His Father loves us, and will not suffer anything to harm us. Concerning the past, we rest in His forgiving love; as to the present, it is bright with His loving fellowship; as to the future, it is brilliant with His expected Advent. This is true of the little as well as of the great. He who saves us from the battle-axe of Satanic temptation, also extracts the thorn of a domestic trial. We may rest in Jesus as to our sick child, as to our business trouble, or as to grief of any kind. He is our Comforter in all things, our Sympathizer in every form of temptation. Have you such all-covering rest? If not, why not? Jesus gives it; why do you not partake of it? Have you something which you could not bring to Him? Then, fly from it; for it is no fit thing for a believer to possess. A disciple should know neither grief nor joy which he could not reveal to his Lord.

This rest, we may conclude, *must be a very wonderful one,* since Jesus gives it. His hands give not by penny-worths and ounces; he gives golden gifts, in quantity immeasurable. It is Jesus who gives the peace of God which passeth all understanding. It is written, " Great peace have they which love Thy law;" what peace must they have who love God's Son! There are periods when Jesus gives us a heavenly Elysium of rest; we cannot describe the divine repose of our hearts at such times. We read, in the Gospels, that when Jesus hushed the storm, "there was a great calm," not simply "a calm", but a great calm, unusual, absolute, perfect, memorable. It reminds us of the stillness which John describes in the Revelation: " I saw four angels standing on the four corners of the earth, holding the four winds of the earth, that the wind should not blow on the earth, nor on the sea, nor on any tree;" not a ripple stirred the waters, not a leaf moved on the trees.

Assuredly, our Lord has given a blessed rest to those who trust Him, and follow Him. They are often unable to inform others as to their deep peace, and the reasons upon which it is founded; but they know it, and it brings them an inward wealth compared with which the fortune of an ungodly millionaire is poverty itself. May we all know to the full, by happy, personal experience, the meaning of our Saviour's promise, " I will give you rest "!

II. But now, in the second place, let us ask, WHY SHOULD WE HAVE THIS REST?

The first answer is in our text. We should enjoy this rest *because Jesus gives it*. As He gives it, we *ought* to take it. Because He gives it, we *may* take it. I have known some Christians who have thought that it would be presumption on their part to take this rest; so they have kept fluttering about, like frightened birds, weary with their long flights, but not daring to fold their tired wings, and rest. If there is any presumption in the case, let us not be so presumptuous as to think that we know better than our Lord. He gives us rest: for that reason, if for no other, let us take it, promptly and gratefully. "Rest in the Lord, and wait patiently for Him." Say with David, "My heart is fixed, O God, my heart is fixed: I will sing and give praise."

> " Now rest, my long-divided heart;
> Fix'd on this blissful centre, rest."

Next, we should take the rest that Jesus gives, *because it will refresh us*. We are often weary; sometimes we are weary *in* God's work, though I trust we are never weary *of* it. There are many things to cause us weariness: sin, sorrow, the worldliness of professors, the prevalence of error in the Church, and so on. Often, we are like a tired child, who can hold up his little head no longer. What does he do? Why, he just goes to sleep in his mother's arms! Let us be as wise as the little one; and let us rest in our loving Saviour's embrace. The poet speaks of—

> " Tired nature's sweet restorer, balmy sleep;"

and so it is. Sometimes, the very best thing a Christian man can do is, literally, to go to sleep. When he wakes, he will be so refreshed, that he will seem to be in a new world. But spiritually, there is no refreshing like that which comes from the rest which Christ gives. As Isaiah said, " This is the rest wherewith ye may cause the weary to rest : and this is the refreshing." Dr. Bonar's sweet hymn, which is so suitable for a sinner coming to Christ for the first time, is just as appropriate for a weary saint returning to his Saviour's arms ; for he, too, can sing,—

> " I heard the voice of Jesus say,
>   ' Come unto Me, and rest ;
>   Lay down, thou weary one, lay down
>   Thy head upon My breast.'
>   I came to Jesus as I was,
>   Weary, and worn, and sad :
>   I found in Him a resting-place,
>   And He has made me glad."

Another reason why we should have this rest is, that *it will enable us to concentrate all our faculties.* Many, who might be strong servants of the Lord, are very weak, because their energies are not concentrated upon one object. They do not say with Paul, " This one thing I do." We are such poor creatures that we cannot occupy our minds with more than one subject at a time. Why, even the buzzing of a fly, or the trumpeting of a mosquito, would be quite sufficient to take our thoughts away from our present holy service! As long as we have any burden resting on our shoulders, we cannot enjoy perfect rest ; and as long as there is any burden on our conscience or heart, we cannot have rest of soul. How are we to be freed from these burdens ? Only by yielding ourselves wholly to the Great Burden-Bearer, who says, " Come unto Me, and

I will give you rest." Possessing this rest, all our faculties will be centred and focussed upon one object, and with undivided hearts we shall seek God's glory.

Having obtained this rest, *we shall be able to testify for our Lord.* I remember, when I first began to teach in a Sunday-school, that I was speaking one day to my class upon the words, " He that believeth on Me hath everlasting life." I was rather taken by surprise when one of the boys said to me, " Teacher, have *you* got everlasting life?" I replied, " I hope so." The scholar was not satisfied with my answer, so he asked another question, " But, teacher, don't you *know*?" The boy was right; there can be no true testimony except that which springs from assured conviction of our own safety and joy in the Lord. We speak that we do know; we believe, and therefore speak. Rest of heart, through coming to Christ, enables us to invite others to Him with great confidence, for we can tell them what heavenly peace He has given to us. This will enable us to put the gospel very attractively, for the evidence of our own experience will help others to trust the Lord for themselves. With the beloved apostle John, we shall be able to say to our hearers, " That which was from the beginning, which we have heard, which we have seen with our eyes, which we have looked upon, and our hands have handled, of the Word of life; (for the life was manifested, and we have seen it, and bear witness, and shew unto you that eternal life, which was with the Father, and was manifested unto us;) that which we have seen and heard declare we unto you, that ye also may have fellowship with us : and truly our fellowship is with the Father, and with His Son Jesus Christ."

Once more, *this rest is necessary to our growth.* The lily in the garden is not taken up and transplanted two or three times a day; that would be the way to prevent all growth. But it is kept in one place, and tenderly nurtured. It is by keeping it quite still that the gardener helps it to attain to perfection. A child of God would grow much more rapidly if he would but rest in one place instead of being always on the move. " In returning and rest shall ye be saved; in quietness and in confidence shall be your strength." Martha was cumbered about much serving; but Mary sat at Jesus' feet. It is not difficult to tell which of them would be the more likely to grow in the grace and knowledge of our Lord Jesus Christ.

This is a tempting theme, but I must not linger over it, as we must come to the communion. I will give only one more answer to the question, " Why should we have this rest ? " *It will prepare us for heaven.* I was reading a book, the other day, in which I met with this expression,—" The streets of heaven begin on earth." That is true; heaven is not so far away as some people think. Heaven is the place of perfect holiness, the place of sinless service, the place of eternal glory; and there is nothing that will prepare us for heaven like this rest that Jesus gives. Heaven must be in us before we are in heaven; and he who has this rest has heaven begun below. Enoch was virtually in heaven while he walked with God on the earth, and he had only to continue that holy walk to find himself actually in heaven. This world is part of our Lord's great house, of which heaven is the upper story. Some of us may hear the Master's call, " Come up higher," sooner than we think; and then, with we rest *in* Christ, there we shall rest *with* Christ. The more we have of this blessed rest now, the better shall we be prepared for the rest that remaineth to the people of God, that eternal "keeping of a Sabbath" in the Paradise above.

III. I have left myself only a minute for the answers to my third question,—HOW CAN WE OBTAIN THIS REST?

First, by *coming to Christ.* He says, "Come unto Me, ... and I will give you rest." I trust that all in this little company have come to Christ by faith; now let us come to Him in blessed fellowship and communion at His table. Let us keep on coming to Him, as the apostle says, "to whom coming," continually coming, and never going away. When we wake in the morning, let us come to Christ in the act of renewed communion with Him; all the day long, let us keep on coming to Him even while we are occupied with the affairs of this life; and at night, let our last waking moments be spent in coming to Jesus. Let us come to Christ by searching the Scriptures, for we shall find Him there on almost every page. Let us come to Christ in our thoughts, desires, aspirations wishes; so shall the promise of the text be fulfilled to us, "I will give you rest."

Next, we obtain rest by *yielding to Christ.* "Take My yoke upon you, ... and ye shall find rest unto your souls." Christ bids us wear *His* yoke, not make one for ourselves. He wants us to share the yoke with Him, to be His true yoke-fellow. It is wonderful that He should be willing to be yoked with us; the only greater wonder is that we should be so unwilling to be yoked with Him. In taking His yoke upon us

190

what joy we shall enter upon our eternal rest ! Here we find rest unto our souls ; a further rest beyond that which He gives us when we come to Him. We first rest in Jesus by faith, and then we rest in Him by obedience. The first rest He gives through His death ; the further rest we find through copying His life.

Lastly, we secure this rest by *learning of Christ.* " Learn of Me, for I am meek and lowly in heart : and ye shall find rest unto your souls." We are to be workers with Christ, taking His yoke upon us ; and, at the same time, we are to be scholars in Christ's school, learning of Him. We are to learn *of* Christ, and to learn *Christ ;* He is both Teacher and lesson. His gentleness of heart fits Him to teach, and makes Him the best illustration of His own teaching. If we can become as He is, we shall rest as He does. The lowly in heart will be restful of heart. Now, as we come to the table of communion, may we find to the full that rest of which we have been speaking, for the Great Rest-Giver's sake ! Amen.